Perfectly Willing

HSING YUN'S HUNDRED SAYINGS SERIES

PERFECTLY WILLING
VENERABLE MASTER HSING YUN

HSI LAI UNIVERSITY PRESS
HACIENDA HEIGHTS, CALIFORNIA

ISBN 0-9642612-0-0
Library of Congress Catalog Card 94-078021

Printed in The United States of America

Contents

Preface

The sutra states:

> Merit from donating the seven treasures
> of the great chiliocosm of three kinds of
> thousands of chiliocosms will not equal
> that attained in upholding a four-line
> verse of wisdom.

What exactly does it mean? There will be the day, the Buddha is telling us, when the riches we donate are exhausted, but the donation of knowledge, skill, truth, and the Dharma treasure is limitless in use and withdrawal.

Sometimes a few words, like a four-line verse, would suffice to impact on an entire life.

I had seen *Universal Gate* magazine seeking readers' submission of one-line verses of wisdom. I had also seen newspapers and periodicals featuring quotable quotes by illustrious characters. Without a doubt, whether it be a mere single-line verse or a few brief words, countless lives could still be touched. Many a time I would feel the urge to share those few words with the greatest influence on me. However, after giving it a little more thought, I realized that, rather than conveying in my own words recollections of the past, I would really want to collect the many words of encouragement given me by those benevolent teachers and gracious acquaintances in my life. The book which resulted would be one way of showing my appreciation to these individuals. Such is the motivation behind *Hsing Yun's Hundred Sayings Series*.

Looking back into the past brings manifold emotions. I remember how, upon hearing Venerable Chih Fêng utter the line: "Don't become the withered bud or rotten seed of Buddhism!" I not only committed myself to the Bodhisattva mind, but also made my Bodhisattva vow; and how, upon hearing Venerable Master Chih K'ai say: "Spread the Dharma to benefit all living beings!" I never let myself forget the formidable responsibility toward humankind that I must shoulder or the mission that my master assigned me.

In my youth, I was once called an underachiever. That drove me to vow to live up to my potentials. Worse, I was deemed useless. But it spurred me on. There was never any doubt in my mind that I can always make up personal weaknesses by added diligence and become a person of worth!

In the days gone by, many encouraged and praised me, or slandered and criticized me. Be they out of kindness or otherwise, their words invariably all became positive causes and conditions along my path toward cultivation. They also formed the favorable and unfavorable — but facilitating — conditions enabling me to learn how to conduct myself in life.

As paddies produce crops of rice, and in mud thrives the immaculate lotus, the state of the objective environment is not nearly as important as our being a healthy seed. For only a good seed produces good fruit. One must allow the springs, summers, autumns, and winters, the winds, frosts, rains, and snows to become causes and conditions of one's growth. Through all objective vicissitudes, we must never lose sight of growth and progress as our purpose in life. Today, I rejoice at being in possession of personal worthiness and virtue, affinity with many people, as well as correct perceptions and knowledge. For this I thank the Buddha's benevolence and the kindly conditions from all ten directions.

In *Hsing Yun's Hundred Sayings Series*, I do not want to indulge in lofty eloquence or see any words and phrases wasted. I only want to contain snippets from my past and my thoughts in the one-line verse from which I have benefited greatly as a verification of the meaning of life. Sometimes I do not feel as if I entirely understand the circumstances in which I find myself. At other times, because of my advanced years and failing memory, remembrances of bygones are beginning to fade. It is those fervent devotees who, by asking to hear about my past, keep prodding me on. I am willing to leave them with some personal reminiscences. That is, while I am still able to speak and write of them. May those disciples who followed me into monasticism find among *Hundred Sayings* some guidelines in life and inspirations for their future.

Starting in July 1992, I began contributing monthly to the *Hundred Sayings* column in *Universal Gate* magazine. The entire collection of *Hundred Sayings* will probably take ten years in all. Completion of such an undertaking — a marathon in life — will have to depend on how long I am able to run, how far I am able to walk!

To date, sixteen pieces out of the hundred were written. To comply with everyone's wishes, these shall go to press,[1] while the rest will wait for another day.

---

[1] The first ten — out of sixteen — articles in the Chinese text are compiled in the first volume of the English translation.

Lastly, I would like to thank *Global News Monthly* and *Universal Gate* magazines for featuring these articles from *Hundred Sayings*, and Reverend Man Kuo, a graduate in accounting from Fu Jen University and a graduate from Fo Kuang Shan Buddhist College, for her help in recording my words. But most of all, I would like to convey my sincerest gratitude to the Triple Gems of all directions and the devotees preserving the Dharma, without whose contributions *Hsing Yun's Hundred Sayings* would simply never be.

> Hsing Yun
> Founder's Quarter,
> Fo Kuang Shan, Taiwan
> August 18, 1993

Acknowledgments

Most in this group have not even met. But in cooperating and adapting to one another's ways, they are bound by the self-same willingness that is perfect. This translated text is the fruition of the shared labor of these individuals: translation and research by Reverend Man I, Jia Du, Christine Kam, May Lui, and Paul Rempel; editing and proof-reading by Edward Little and Amy Lui-Ma; typesetting and formatting by Reverend Hui Chih, Tanya Evanoff, and Helen Tsai; book design and art direction by Anthony Ma; and developmental editing and production coordinating by Reverend Man Ho, with valued advice and support from Reverend Man Hua of International Buddhist Progress Society, R.O.C.

PERFECTLY WILLING

I respect Man Ch'êng,[1] my Dharma brother, for his endurance, his generosity, his great-hearted speech, and his open mind, and hence have kept firmly in mind his saying: "Perfectly willing."

Master Chih K'ai had two disciples, Man Ch'êng and myself. Prior to studying with Master Chih K'ai, Man Ch'êng had followed a different master. This caused him to often remark that he was only half a disciple [to Master Chih K'ai]. Man Ch'êng had experienced a harder time in his youth than I had. Honest and not too smart, he was often bullied and wronged. Like a daughter-in-law in old China, he had to do extra work and took extra blame. Sometimes, seeing that he had taken too many reproaches, I would go and try to console him. Somehow he would always say calmly, "That's all right. I'm perfectly willing to do what I do."

Perfectly Willing to be an Ascetic Monk

During the ten years of my Buddhist study

[1] All Chinese names in this text are romanized by the Wade-Giles system except for a few that are established in Pin-yin.

and discipline, I had also been subjected to many ruthless reproaches and unreasonable requests. Rigid and closed, Buddhist monastic training not only kept us sequestered from the outside world but also restricted what we could see and hear. To look around and talk freely were forbidden. For a young and curious boy there could be no greater test than this. Also, the lack of basic necessities and arduousness of labor were beyond imagination. I lived through these hardships with a peaceful mind, not taking the difficulties as suffering. The motto that supported me was, as Man Ch'êng used to say: "I'm perfectly willing." I am perfectly willing to become a Buddhist monk, perfectly willing to study, perfectly willing to be an ascetic, and perfectly willing to accept all blame and wrong. Thus I lived those ten years in serenity. The tenacity and perseverance cultivated during that period were strong assets in my efforts to propagate Buddhism years later.

At twenty-one I left the monastery to be principal in a country primary school. Although I was totally inexperienced in educational administration, I worked diligently with an open-minded, persistent, perfectly willing, and humble attitude, and did quite well at my first position.

I was twenty-two and in charge of Hua-ts'ang Temple in Nanjing. The impossible situation that the country was in made me realize that there was little possibility of Buddhism becoming widely accepted then. Still, with the knowledge that I might lose my life, I along with others published *Nu-t'ao* (Raging Billows),[2] a monthly publication advocating revolutionary thoughts in the hope of saving our faith. Time and again we found ourselves in extremely dangerous situations but were always perfectly willing to sacrifice for our cause. The more we were deterred, the bolder and more determined we became.

Perfectly Willing Despite Ridicule

When I first arrived in Taiwan, people everywhere were restless and distrustful. All my attempts to seek shelter at different temples failed. Getting basic necessities such as food and shelter became a serious problem. Although *Chin-jih ching-nien* (Today's Youth) and *K'an-chan jih-pao* (Wartime Daily) had offered me positions as editor and reporter, I decided, after some serious consideration, that

[2] All publication titles in this text are given first in transliteration and then translation in brackets unless stated otherwise.

I would be what a monk should be and not put the incidental before the fundamental. Therefore, I declined both offers. Many nights I spent cold and hungry. So many ridiculed me as obsolete, sluggish, and unknowing of the affairs of our time. Yet I was perfectly willing to do what a monk should.

Finally I settled in a temple, doing all kinds of hard labor from early in the morning to late at night. Although I was very busy with many tasks, such as dragging a cart to buy groceries, carrying firewood and water, tending the garden, traveling long distances to collect rent, cleaning the temple, and burying the dead, I was grateful for the shelter and was perfectly willing to reciprocate the temple's kindness with hard labor.

My daily chores completed, I wrote articles to propagate Buddhism. The articles called for a reformed practice of Buddhism, speaking against government interference in religion and suggesting laws be established to assure equal treatment for all religions, and were sent to various newspapers. During those years I had nothing but enthusiasm for and devotion in Buddhism.

Often I would see other monks coming back from services with loads of contributions while I could not even afford the ink and paper that I needed for writing. But I was never envious of anybody because my ultimate goal was to promote Buddhism and serve others.

One day as I was writing, a woman who had often volunteered at the temple came up to me and said kindly, "You must go and look for work, otherwise you'll end up starving." I later found out that, whenever I was buried in reading and writing papers, I drew curious looks from people around the temple. Men of letters in those days were not quite highly regarded. Nonetheless, I insisted that articles and letters were indispensable in advocating and spreading Buddhism. Writing for Central Broadcasting Station and various journals might have driven me to the brink of starvation, but then, I was perfectly willing to continue what I did.

Perfectly Willing to Spread the Dharma

To assist Venerable Master Tung Ch'u in editing *Jên-shêng yüeh-k'an* (Life Monthly), I paid from my own pocket for paper and postage and for transportation. This continued for more than six years. To help publish *Chin-jih Fo-chiao* (Buddhism Today), I commuted often between Taipei and Ilan on an empty stomach and spent countless sleepless nights composing articles. I never took this as suffering. I was determined that for Buddhism I would always be perfectly willing to dedicate everything, even my own life.

In the years when few people were willing to work for the Buddhist culture, I was especially grateful to those intellectuals who had helped me. To them, I would pay my ultimate respect and offer any service I could render. For those who shared my interest in writing, I was never too tired or short for time to provide instruction, and was always happy to do so.

Even today I continue to work with friends in publishing on Buddhist works. When Larui Cheng wanted to publish the imperial collection of Buddhist sutras, I volunteered to approach Chin Hsiao-yi, curator of the National Palace Museum, for it. I helped Yao Chia-yen of Literate Publishing distribute his Buddhist titles. I advised and sponsored Chang Man-tao and Chu Chiang-yuan, whom I did not know well, in publishing two series, *Hsien-tai Fo-chiao hsüeh-shu ts'ung-k'an* (*Contemporary Buddhist Texts Compiled in One Hundred Books*) and *Shih-chieh Fo-chiao ming-chu fan-i lun-ts'ung* (Translations from World Classics in

Buddhism Series). I raised funds to help them survive financial crises. Much against those who disapproved, I was perfectly willing in my efforts to salvage these two publications, which have since made marked contributions to the advancement of Buddhism.

Over thirty years, from publishing journals like *Awaken the World* and *Universal Gate*, compiling *Fo Kuang Buddhist Canon*, distributing *Fo Kuang Buddhist Dictionary*, and establishing Buddhist Cultural Center and Fo Kuang Publishing House, the cultural endeavors in Fo Kuang Shan had encountered many financial problems. But these shortages never affected my determination.

I saved from food allowances and personal expenses to acquire and collect Buddhist cultural artifacts. To cut shipping costs, I carried heavy Buddhist statues, instruments, and scripts in my luggage. I often was met with curious stares and a few times was mistaken for a character dabbling in the trading of cultural articles. To stay on course, I was perfectly willing to bear all such embarrassment and smears. As a result some ten libraries were built in Taiwan and abroad. Buddhist museums at Fo Kuang Shan, Hsi Lai Temple, and Paris Vihara were completed. For the rapidly increasing Buddhist followers, I was perfectly willing to bear any financial burden.

Perfectly Willing to Cultivate the Buddhist Community

Coming a long way from an era of chaos and uncertainty, and seeing that the people in Taiwan were yet to be enlightened and that Buddhism had yet to prosper, I came to be aware of the importance of education more than ever. On completion of Shou-shan Temple, I decided to establish there an institute for the purpose of educating the Buddhist community. Many of my disciples became greatly concerned over our financial ability to cover food and shelter, let alone the whole of the institute. But the urgency of education drove me to decide that, even left penniless and compelled to beg like Wu Hsün for the cause of education, I would be perfectly willing. Whenever I had saved enough, I would buy furniture and stationery for the institute and hire learned scholars to come and teach. Later, to establish Eastern Buddhist College, I stayed up all night holding Buddhist services — a practice I normally do not favor. To prepare for the construction of Chinese Buddhist Research Institute, I together with my disciples worked long and hard on food sales to raise funds. I would not hesitate to hire excellent scholars from overseas to come and teach English Buddhist courses in the English Buddhist program of the international academic department. Colleagues in our accounting department were often disheartened by the lack of funds. I was certainly aware of our restrictions. But so long as competent human resources in the Buddhist community continued to be strengthened and Buddhism be propagated worldwide, I would always be perfectly willing to sacrifice and contribute.

Training programs for novice monks were even harder to run. It took great efforts to raise boys in early adolescence to become learned Buddhists. After their military service, many of them gave in to the temptations of society and never returned to the temple. Whenever this happened, my heart would ache as if from a tremendous loss. But as long as young people would apply themselves to the Buddhist education, I would happily take them in. My disciples, not wanting to see me disappointed, would often tell me, "These kids won't ever remember what you've done for them!" My response that I was perfectly willing often left them wordless in disagreement.

Twenty years have passed, and only a few are left from my original group of fifty novice monks. Hui Lung, Hui Chun, Hui Tsang, and Hui Shang are playing important roles now in Fo Kuang Shan. Hui Lung is the executive officer in charge of the charitable foundation. Hui Chun, innovative in the propagation of Buddhism, is a member of Fo Kuang Shan's religious affairs committee. Although I have plowed more than harvested, I am satisfied. There are currently over a hundred members in the training program for novice monks — three times as many as when I first started — but then again how many will stay for good? Still, I am perfectly willing to teach them.

Twenty-nine years ago, Venerables Nan Ting, Wu Yi, and myself established Chih-kuang School of Commerce. Later, my name ceased to appear in business correspondences and official documents. I was not even allowed to send representatives to their meetings. Some thought it unfair but I would only respond with a smile.

There were countless setbacks in my attempts to promote Buddhist education. When in 1980 I set up the Graduate School of Indian Culture at Chinese Culture University, I had to lecture as well as travel back and forth to raise funds. After three school terms, Chang

Chi-yun, the founder, died, and the program was discontinued. My efforts, once again, fell fruitless. Not the least upset, I continued to be perfectly willing to educate gifted Buddhists. Eventually the university president wanted to see the study of Buddhism reestablished and asked me time and again to reopen the graduate school: the light of truth will always shine!

Today Buddhist education centers include Hsi Lai University and many Chinese schools overseas, as well as six Buddhist colleges and P'u Men High School in Taiwan. Fo Kuang University is about to be instituted, and I must work on its planning. I keep reminding myself, "For the sake of education, I shall always be perfectly willing to face adversities and challenges of all forms."

The cause of education, after all, sees no immediate results but takes years of hard work. I used to exhaust myself preparing for Buddhist lectures. I confronted the authorities fighting for freedom to spread Buddhism. I preached using innovative modern techniques, only to be criticized by conservatives. And I had resorted to belt-tightening to save for lecture tours far and wide.

Perfectly Willing to Go Far and Wide

At twenty-eight I went on a lecture tour to the eastern part of Taiwan. To save on shipping expenses, I lugged around a heavy projector all the time. This resulted in serious arthritis. Somehow, when the doctor told me I might lose my legs, I was neither afraid nor regretful because I was perfectly willing to do what I could to spread Buddhism. And I thought losing my legs might even enable me to spend more time reading and writing while still advocating Buddhism. At the time I was so engaged in my work that I forgot about the disease. Magically, it went away and I recovered.

I continued to travel every week between Ilan and Kaohsiung to lecture for ten years. I went on foot to remote temples. As the years went by, invitations to lecture took up so much of my schedule that I got used to eating and sleeping in cars and on planes, and traveling across the miles from continent to continent. Even after retirement from Fo Kuang Shan eight years ago, I still attend meetings. Whenever there is a request, I will always be there.

When I decided to establish Fo Kuang
Shan years ago, my disciples were all
discouraged by the thorns and thistles
covering the hills. They thought that with
Shou-shan Temple established, another temple
in which to hold Buddhist lectures and
activities was not necessary. The idea of
building temples overseas was not favored by
many either. Their objections might be valid,
but I still felt that, in order to provide a home
for Buddhist disciples and deliverance for the
people, I would be perfectly willing to take on
any hard tasks.

After Fo Kuang Shan was founded, we
helped build local roads and bridges,
established schools and charity programs, and
contributed diligently toward community
development. However, some villagers
wanted more. A few of these even hurt monks
and defamed Buddhism. Some people
complained about spending on temples
outside Taiwan, not realizing that these
temples are really generous gifts to the rest of
the world. In poverty Taiwan had once
received aid from the United States. Now that
things have changed for the better for us, it
should be our turn to be a generous giver. How
deplorable that some of us should be so

greedy, angry, and ignorant! Duty-bound in the spread of Buddhism and with no regrets, I was perfectly willing to tolerate all such slanders.

In sheer enthusiasm, I have lectured on Buddhist principles using the most modern methods available, managed temples in a democratic way, related Buddhism with real life, and taken Buddhism to an international stature. In willingness and compassion, I strive for the goals of relieving suffering, bringing happiness, and benefiting all beings. With humbleness, I provide guidance to everyone. I am concerned with the affairs of the country and would not hesitate to speak for the people. Believers and political figures alike I would entertain with respect at the temple. I would just as gladly offer lectures to the military.

On those clear nights in self-reflection, I realize that for Buddhism and the sangha I have done my best, and for my country and the people I have given every effort. For all my mere intentions, I have never expected to be appreciated and, least of all, to be called the "business monk" or the "political monk." Nonetheless, I am perfectly willing to bear it all along a broader path for the spread of Buddhism.

Perfectly Willing to Raise Successors

Some people envy me for my daily increasing disciples, but few realize the hardships behind. The *Vimalakīrti Sutra* states:

> All the passions are the disciples,
> Controlled at will.

I console, encourage, and lecture my followers, all of different personalities. I solve their problems and provide them with the appropriate environment in which to learn, opportunities for further study, quiet and peaceful accommodation, and various other facilities and benefits. I protect and care for them, like I would tend a delicate orchid. It is certainly a pleasure to see that many become appreciative, but I am always saddened most by those who break with their faith. I remember supporting two sisters while they attended medical school ten years ago. They ended up not only failing to contribute but also sneering at other disciples. Some followers, upon becoming educated, turned arrogant and went to work for other organizations. Rather than being concerned over efforts wasted and hopes destroyed, I worry most about their well-being: once outside the mountain gate, will they lose their way in the secular world?

Fortunately, I have many outstanding disciples who have dedicated their lives to Buddhism and to the people. Hsin Ping, kind and generous, was perfectly willing to follow me in the early years of Fo Kuang Shan. Now the abbot, he has taken over all responsibilities and debts since my retirement. Always determined and never discouraged, he has never regretted committing himself to this life. Tzu Chuang, gentle and patient, went in pumps from household to household to deliver Buddhist texts forty years ago before she became a Buddhist nun. Later she went to Hsi Lai Temple in America and spent ten hard years building and strengthening it. She has always been perfectly willing to take responsibilities and accept blame. Talented Tzu Hui gave up a well-paying job to be my interpreter in the propagation of Buddhism. She had also taught at the university. Tzu Jung, competent and experienced, has been perfectly willing in assuming the responsibility of spreading Buddhism and benefiting people since becoming a Buddhist in 1953. Despite her physical fragility, she remains in charge of Buddha's Light International Association, Republic of China, working hard with little rest. Tzu Chia, in her serenity, has been perfectly willing in dedicating herself to educating sangha members in the monasteries for thirty years since her return from studying in Japan. There are also Tzu Yi, Hsin Ting, Yi Yen, Yi Heng, Hui Kai, Yi Kung, Yi Ti, Yi Chun, and Yi Fa as well as others from later years, such as Man Cheng, who is perfectly willing to work in Nepal, Man Jen, an American nun who is perfectly willing to clean and beautify Fo Kuang Shan, and Lee In-ok from Korea, who is perfectly willing to come and serve at Buddha's Light International Association, Republic of China, since her graduation from National Cheng Kung University. To all aspiring Buddhist disciples, I would urge you to be perfectly willing to dedicate yourself. Maintain a perfectly willing attitude as you strive for your goals. All hardships and obstacles will then mean nothing. All restrictions in life will be undone. There will be little that cannot be attained, and no wishes will be left unfulfilled.

A WORLD OF
NOT LOOKING AND
NOT LISTENING

Oツne who truly knows how to listen listens to the sound of silence. One who genuinely knows how to look looks at the inner world.

The sagacity was Ch'an master Ming Tu's, supervisor of the meditation hall where I occasionally meditated during my early days at the Buddhist college.

I did not understand the statement very well at the time, but I kept it in mind, having a feeling that embedded in it were profound Dharma meanings. I could not have guessed then that it would come to cast an enormous influence on my later life.

View the World with the Mind's Eyes

At fifteen I went for the Triple Platform ordination. As I inquisitively browsed around, there came a hard stick sharply down on my body.

"What are you looking at?" asked the preceptor. "What in the world belongs to you?"

At his words I closed my eyes and stopped looking. In a world of darkness, I lit a light in my mind, finding everything on earth right there — in my mind. I learned to look inward, not outward; at the nonexisting, not the existing; at the real, not the illusory; at myself, not others.

Walking down a long corridor three months later, I opened my eyes again. The sights — green hills and bodies of water, and white clouds in a clear blue sky — were too beautiful to be fully appreciated. After a period of self-reflection, the hills and water were still the same as I had seen them, but the feelings I had were much different from what they had been in the past. To this day, I can still walk in the dark or climb stairs in ease — without using my eyes. Things in the world would be much more accurately perceived if we use our minds', instead of our physical, eyes.

When we purchased Fo Kuang Shan twenty-eight years ago, the devotees despaired of the massive weeds, thorny bushes, and impossible transportation. Many asked, "Who will ever want to come here?" Despite such views I led the monastics to work. Together we lugged rocks, conveyed dirt, cleared hills, and filled dikes, eventually creating a Buddhist haven out of the wilderness. Today Fo Kuang Shan has become not only a major tourist attraction in Taiwan but also a prominent international center of Buddhism. Those who were initially reluctant to come have returned many, many times. This experience but indicates what we first see with our eyes might not be correct. Determination assures success; we must be resolute.

Heed the Buddha's Voice

After my ordination in 1941 I studied at an ordinance college. While on night patrol I would listen to leaves brushing against the bricks and insects buzzing in the still air. One night, as I paused to hear the slight sounds in the stillness, a staff landed unexpectedly on my back.

"What are you listening to?" shouted the disciplinary officer. "Cover your ears. What on earth should you be listening to?"

At that admonishment I began to practice abstinence from listening, but that was terribly difficult. I had to stuff my ears with cotton balls at first in order not to hear the sounds around me. Gradually, my hearing organs became purer, and my mind, brighter.

Just as I was beginning to appreciate the serenity of silence, I was slapped again.

"Why did you stuff your ears with

cotton?" asked the instructor. "Open your ears and listen! What sounds shouldn't you be hearing?"

I removed the cotton balls; all kinds of noises dashed through the air and pierced my brain. After a while I became calmer and more collected, and came to recognize many wonderful sounds in nature. I realized how I had misused my ears in the past. I resolved from then on only to listen to genuine words, not rumors; to good words, not slander; to the Buddhist Dharma, not triviality; to truth, not falsities.

Fifty years later, I returned home in the Chinese New Year of 1993 to visit my mother. Zhao Pu-chu, president of the Buddhist Association of China, came from Beijing to Nanjing to greet me. During a delightful conversation, his wife, much amazed, commented, "My husband is hard of hearing and often can't hear what others say. How come he could hear everything that Venerable Master Hsing Yun said today?" Zhao replied, "My ears only listen to words that need to be heard, not those that need not be." Hear without listening; listen without hearing — such is the epitome of the art of hearing and listening.

I once had an experience in listening

without hearing. It took place in 1954 during a seven-day retreat at Lei-yin Temple in Ilan. Amidst the continual recitation of the Buddha's name, I allowed myself to become immersed in the serenity of meditation and the Pureland. Every moment of those seven days, I sensed the continuity of the chanting. When I was away from the Buddha hall, in my mind the chanting still lingered. Every mouthful at mealtime was charged with "Amitabha Buddha! Amitabha Buddha!" Even the sound of teeth-brushing became an utterance of "Amitabha Buddha." Everything I was engaged in and every moment of thought were filled with the name "Amitabha Buddha." Seven days of retreat slipped by like a moment. The experience — transcending the duality of self and others, a unified state of mind, and the absence of space and time — remains vivid to this day.

Enhance Wisdom Through Serenity

While attending Chiao-shan Buddhist College at nineteen, I attempted to observe silence. It was difficult at first. At times, out of neglect, I would speak. When that happened, I would remove myself to the back of the main hall,

face the island across the water, and slap
myself across the mouth until it bled. A year
went by. My mouth was emptied of voices,
and my mind freed of defiling thoughts. In
silence I was able to observe total liberty for
all beings. Time seemed to stretch, as did finite
space.

I came to comprehend the meaning of the
statement: "A split second is all of eternity." I
knew the feeling of "encompassing the
universe in the infinitesimal." At the end of
my observance of silence, I spoke again. My
classmates were amazed at the swiftness of my
reactions. It reminded me of my
grandmother's pickled vegetables: the tighter
she sealed the jar, the more luscious the pickles
became. Humans are not any different. We
chase after sights and sounds all the time, our
minds unable to be set on the Buddhist path.
There is a saying: "Serenity leads a long way."
In serenity alone — not looking, listening, or
speaking improperly — are we able to
rediscover ourselves, enhance our wisdom, see
what others have not seen, hear what others
have not heard, and say what others have not
said.

Once in Japan in 1963 I spotted the figures
of three monkeys sculpted on the beams of the
Tōshōgun in Nikko National Park. One

monkey had its hands over its eyes; the second, over its ears; and the third, over its mouth. I paused for a moment, and an understanding struck me. Our six sense organs — eyes, ears, nose, tongue, body, and mind — constantly cling to objects in the external world. We distinguish the six sense objects — sights, sounds, odors, tastes, feelings, and thoughts — which give rise to vexations. If we constantly reflect on ourselves, not allowing our minds to roam, and if we restrain ourselves from looking at, listening to, and uttering what ought not to be seen, heard, or said, illusions will cease to arise, as will karma, ignorance, and vexations.

Twenty years ago I invited Yu Kuo-chi to teach music at the Buddhist college. On his recommendation we purchased a state-of-the-art sound system to facilitate better instruction. He was playing a number of symphonic pieces on the first day of class when, suddenly, the sounds of a gusty wind, lightning, and galloping horses blasted from the speakers and filled the classroom. When it was over, he excitedly asked the students, "Of the pieces you just heard, which one sounded best to you?" Reverend Yi Heng, a student at the time, rose and replied, "Sir, the best part was when it ended."

Lao Tzu once remarked: "The five colors blind one; the five notes deafen one." The world's multifarious sights and sounds blind, deafen, and disorient us. In order to settle our lives, we must penetrate the formless phenomenon, listen to the sound of silence, and speak the wordless speech.

Utilize Our Eyes, Ears, and Tongue

No forms and no sounds. Yet we can still lead a remarkable life in a world filled with sights and sounds. I used to distribute flyers and put up posters in the streets in wartime China to propagate reform in Buddhism. Circumstances were life-threatening, but I only had the future of Buddhism in my eyes and the agonized cries of souls in my ears. I did not see any weapons or hear any bombing.

I had led many groups on pilgrimages, and noticed that people would often chat while the guide made announcements. Some would want to do things their own way and blame others when things went wrong. They would ignore a sign that gave clear directions and ask for verbal instructions instead. A common problem of modern humanity is such that we use the mouth a lot but the eyes and ears only a little.

Many not only underestimate the functions of the eyes and ears, but also know not how to properly look with their eyes, listen with their ears, and speak with their mouths even if they use them. Big Buddha's Land in Fo Kuang Shan is well-known worldwide; thousands come to visit everyday. However, some people, seeing that the statues are made of cement, would dismiss them as elements of a worthless concrete culture. Their derision aside, I have seen nothing but sacred statues of the Buddha for over twenty years at Fo Kuang Shan. How is it that some people only notice the cement and do not see the Buddhas? Looking in itself is inadequate; we should penetrate deeply, investigate thoroughly, and listen well.

My grandmother had been a devout Buddhist since she was seventeen. Although she was kind and gentle, she lost some of her grandchildren when they were only three or four years of age. She never cried or complained, and simply ignored neighbors' gossips. Some might have wondered if she had any feelings or if she loved her grandchildren at all. If people should wonder about her feelings, they were wrong! A Buddhist most of her life, she understood life: life and death are but parts of living; the law of karma is sound and clear. That was the reason why she could face adversity without upset or exasperation.

Observe with a Carefree State of Mind

When I first arrived in Taiwan, I had a tough time looking for a place to stay. I wandered around and spent many days in destitution. However, those experiences helped better my appreciation of the verse:

Sounds of the stream are
     words of the Dharma;
Mountain scenes are nothing but
     the pure Dharma body.

It filled my heart with joy. I sometimes encountered ridicule and persecution when preaching in the community. I was never upset because hardship to me is a facilitating and encouraging means. Hardship is a part of life; when overcome, the true meaning of happiness will be better cherished. The best fruit comes from hard work and diligence; hence I have always found life to be joyful.

Once I caught a terrible cold and lost my voice. In my calm I thought to myself, "It's not bad to be dumb. Of all people on earth, a

mute is least likely to say the wrong thing."
Another time a doctor told me that my legs
had to be amputated because of severe
arthritis. "If I can't get around as easily, I can,
then, spend more time studying and writing,"
I told myself and remained at ease.

If we can conceive the immense
conglomeration of this complex and
multifarious world in the terms of the Buddhist
principles, we will remain carefree no matter
what we see in people, happenings, things,
surroundings, principles, and minds. Every
experience will be free of hindrances, fears, and
misinterpretations. We will, right at that very
moment, become Bodhisattva Avalokiteśvara,
the Bodhisattva of Carefree Observance, and
need to search outward no more.

The same applies to listening. To be able
to listen attentively is still not perfect. We must
learn to listen well, and to transform bad words
into good ones, and perversion into
righteousness. People ask how I would apply
the Buddha's teachings in daily life. I learn
the most about Buddhism through everyday
activities, interpersonal dealings, and coping
with mundane matters. In fact it was from an
instructor who could not teach that I learned
to teach. The Buddhist college in the past was

not too particular about teaching methods. But I would watch the way a teacher instructed his class, listen carefully, and try putting myself in his place. Gradually, teaching Buddhism became a part of me. Whether listening to or giving a Buddhist lecture, I would apply the Four Reliances which the Buddha taught to guide my study: rely on the Dharma, not the person; on the meaning, not the words; on the definitive meaning, not the interpretive; on the direct, intuitive knowledge of reality, not the discursive thoughts. In this way, I was able to comprehend, absorb, and digest the teachings, retaining the essence and ridding my mind of the unnecessary. Everything in the world may become part of my treasure in that way.

Many times my disciples told me that I am expert in solving interpersonal disputes, and that any problem can be minimized or reduced to nothing in my hands. I do listen patiently to complaints and give situations a thorough analysis. Most important of all, I listen to both sides of a story. I do not conclude based on one-sided information; nor do I judge based on a moment alone. If a person is able to listen attentively and hear all sides, judgment will not be flawed!

Everything is Impermanent

After forty years away from home, I could not find the way around my own village when I returned. Sometimes I might leave Fo Kuang Shan for a mere fortnight and notice changes upon return. What we see and hear are manifestations of the principle of dependent origination and the void nature of things. Everything appears or disappears depending on the aggregation or dissipation of necessary causes and conditions. Nothing is permanent; the nature of true form is formless.

Someone once asked a question at a seminar: "What does Fo Kuang Shan look like?" Some compared it to the five fingers of a hand or the petals of an orchid; others suggested a traditional monastery or a modern temple. In my opinion, all the respondents were both right and wrong. When I founded Fo Kuang Shan, I did not have a set plan. I merely built when the causes and conditions were right. That is why Fo Kuang Shan is made up of buildings of different kinds and encompasses a wide variety of activities. It is such a magnificent conglomeration because a mold was never cast. Some disciples complain about the current constructions and that it is not as quiet as it used to be. But to me, this is progress. I hear no noise; Fo Kuang Shan is as peaceful and serene as it has always been.

Since retiring from the position of abbot, invitations to lecture, visits from Buddhists overseas, and the teaching of disciples have kept me just as busy. Although the days go by as if I am scrambling for every second, my state of mind has become brighter and emptier. I am always among people and amidst happenings. But in a conversation or while conducting business, I can still enjoy the scenery, edit and write articles, outline lectures, and make plans for the continued development of Buddhism. There are no persons or matters in my mind.

Experience Wonderful Truth in Void

Many times I wake up not knowing where I am. It feels as if I have forgotten who I am. Others keep telling me that I am too busy and that I should rest more. But I do not feel busy at all. Praise or insult, gain or loss, have or have-not, coming or going, hungry or full, morning or evening, it does not matter; I do not cling.

Helen Keller, blind in her eyes but not in her mind, was a great educator. Beethoven,

33

deaf in his ears but not in his mind, composed many melodious masterworks. Ch'an master Tê Shan Hsüan Chien was enlightened when Lung T'an Ch'ung Hsin extinguished the lamp. Five thousand Bodhisattvas came to the realization of the nonarising nature of all dharmas as a result of Vimalakīrti's silence. I, not virtuous or wise, regret to say that I have accomplished nothing comparable. But from the bottom of my heart I am grateful to Buddhism for teaching me the wonderful truth of silence, formlessness, and wordlessness. This teaching has enabled me to constantly serve the sentient beings while living in Ch'an joy, not to feel pained in suffering or hard-pressed under pressure.

A Ch'an master once said:

> Live freely and be carefree; go with the flow. Maintain a mind of equanimity; do not cling to attaining.

If we can apply this advice in our lives, we will be living in a world of not looking and not listening.

A THOUSAND YEARS
IN ONE MOMENT;
ONE MOMENT IN
A THOUSAND YEARS

In 1989 I visited mainland China. President of the Buddhist Association of China, Zhao Pu-chu, came to the airport to greet me. When we met, he said, "This is truly a thousand years in one moment, and one moment in a thousand years!" What he meant was profound. I left mainland China more than forty years ago; into two worlds the Strait of Taiwan has separated us. This encounter both picked up where the past left off and made way for the future. Indeed a thousand years went past in one moment, and one moment, in a thousand years. Pondering this life of mine, the chain of events was like smoke and dust. I see in every one of them a thousand years in one moment, and one moment in a thousand years.

At twelve, when the average child would be laughing and playing, I became a monk out of a casual promise that I had made. A moment's causes and conditions brought me a lifetime's immersion in the sea of the Dharma and gathering of the limitless truth of Buddhism.

In my youth I never ceased to gather knowledge and understanding at old monasteries in famous mountains. Gradually molding my character under an orthodox monastic education, I also came in contact with many virtuous and eminent masters. Day by day I nurtured notions of enlightenment and the life of wisdom under their constant personal instructions. Drops of the Dharma dew from that period accumulated into the surge of a great current, bursting through any and all trials and tribulations. Each time I think of this I cannot but cry out inside: "A thousand years in one moment; one moment in a thousand years!"

A Moment's Realization.
Seize the Moment

Ch'i-hsia Shan (Cloud Dwelling Mountain), where I entered the monastic life, embraces the majestic Ch'ien-fo Ling (Thousand Buddhas Range) and the charming Ming-ching Hu (Clear Mirror Lake). In the brightness of the lake and colors of the mountains, and the countless changes that the scenery exhibits, the sublimed oneness of heaven and earth is fully comprehensible. The profundity of "a thousand years in one moment; one moment in a thousand years" is lost in speechlessness.

Each year on the first day of the second

lunar month when I face the congregation of devotees at Fo Kuang Shan, what I feel at heart is ineffable. As countless believers converge, many would pledge not to return because they either slept poorly or did not eat well. Still the following year they come back for no other reason than that it is a thousand years in one moment, and one moment in a thousand years.

There is a saying which goes:

In a single flower one may see the world;
In a single leaf one may see the Buddha.

In all the plants and trees on Fo Kuang Shan can be found a history which reveals the message, "a thousand years in one moment; one moment in a thousand years." Once, after a typhoon, I surveyed the grounds only to find one Bodhi tree beside Treasure Bridge split into two by the winds. I lifted it, supported it with bamboo props, and cared for it with all my heart. Now it has flourished into a tall, shady tree. Another handsome and erect Bodhi tree beside Dragon Pavilion was originally no more than a rootless trunk and branches strewn across the ground. When quite by chance I passed by and saw it, my heart grew sympathetic. I planted it back in the soil, and watered and cared for it each and every day. As if by miracle, it not only took root and sprouted but has also matured into its present luxuriant form.

The "Return to the Epoch of the Buddha" Dharma function, having started in northern Taiwan and passing through the central region until reaching the south, was an extraordinarily ardent affair. When thousands of faithful men and women chanted to the Buddha in praise, the great conference at Gṛdhrakūṭa Mountain (Vulture Peak)[1] seemed to have been reenacted! In one moment were contained 2,500 years of time and space, and the boundless Dharma joy in my heart thoroughly described.

At the Dr. Sun Yat-sen's Memorial Hall and Chung Cheng Cultural Center, ten thousand neophytes assembled to vow to take refuge in the Triple Gems, to sever themselves from the boundless vexations of mundane existence, and to achieve supreme Buddhahood. Their resolve to follow the Buddha's path gave them transport across the river of transmigration. It also injected immeasurable hope into the ideal to purify society. Its impact was, truthfully speaking, a thousand years in one moment, and one moment in a thousand years. I felt the same

[1] An assembly where many sentient beings gathered to listen to the Buddha's preaching of the Dharma.

intensity holding seminars in Hong Kong's Hunghom Coliseum and Malaysia's Dewan Tengku Abdul Rahman, where I witnessed the undivided concentration on the faces of the crowds and listened to their hearty laughter.

Leading the life of a monk for fifty years, when every dawn and dusk is signaled by the sounds of the bell and drum and with every prostration, I never cease to pray and wish for the sound of the bell to spread through all nations and the Dharma to be propagated through the great chiliocosm of three kinds of thousands of chiliocosms. For in everything is a thousand years in one moment, and one moment in a thousand years.

Speak What Should be. Practice What Should be

In 1989 I returned to mainland China. Leaders of the Communist regime, Yang Shang-kun and Li Xien-nien, graciously allowed me to express my views on their religious policy. I urged that museum and forestry personnel be removed from monasteries, and Buddhist places of worship and relics damaged during the Cultural Revolution be returned and repaired. On behalf of countless Buddhists and for the survival of Buddhism, taking on these leaders was a matter of a thousand years in one moment, and one moment in a thousand years.

Back in Taiwan, I had urged the ruling Kuomingtang to exercise magnanimity toward and tolerance of dissidents. No force can obstruct development, freedom, and democracy, all gigantic wheels of changing times. I urged them to let the chain of interrelated changes be and to yield to the desire of the people in order to ensure the support of the masses. I recommended that the government liberalize itself, permit the founding of a Buddhist university, and allow free propagation of the Dharma. The government did eventually open up; there came freedom of religion; also, the university took form. Plucking up the courage to utter those constructive words was to me a matter of a thousand years in one moment, and one moment in a thousand years. Visiting with the king of Thailand, I recommended that he allow the propagation of Mahayana Buddhism in his country. Once the president of the Philippines told me that he wanted Buddhism and Roman Catholicism alike to prosper there. At the inauguration of Buddha's Light International Association, the president of the Commonwealth of Dominica personally invited me to spread the Buddhist faith in his country. During the inauguration of Hsi Lai Temple, a representative from the U.S. president, Ronald Reagan, made a congratulatory address. All these were occasions of a thousand years in one moment, and one moment in a thousand years.

The sixteenth World Fellowship of Buddhists conference was held at Hsi Lai Temple: the real Dharma had finally come to the West! For the first time, the Dharma masters and laity from Beijing and Taipei shook hands and exchanged joyous words in the interest of reunifying China.

The government of the United States has made May 16 "American Buddha's Light Day." Australia donated to International Buddhist Association of Australia twenty-six acres of land for its site. The mayor of Brisbane assisted me in devising a plan to build International Buddhist Association of Queensland. The monastery built by the Archbishop of London, England is used as Fo Kuang Shan's London-based Buddhist center. A thirteenth-century castle in France now houses Fo Kuang Shan's Paris Vihara. South Africa gave six acres of land to Fo Kuang Shan for a temple. As the light of the Buddha shines in every corner of the earth and the water of the Dharma flows over the five continents, these happenings were a thousand years in one moment, and one moment in a thousand years.

One Moment Spanning a Thousand Years

In my entire life I have never received a single diploma, but I know not how many diplomas I gave out. I have never studied in a university, but I taught for many years in universities. I am also a degree examiner with the Ministry of Education and the first monk to have been honored by the education authorities in Taiwan. Too many medals and plaques from district and provincial governments were bestowed on me through the years.

But who am I, anyway? An ordinary monk. A farmer's offspring. Always overwhelmed. All the awards and honors are to me achievements of a thousand years in one moment, and one moment in a thousand years.

From each grain of sand and each piece of stone an ornate mansion is built; with each flower and each tree a courtyard is beautified. All is the result of causes and conditions; all is attributed to the parents, elders, and masses from all directions. The glory belongs to the

Buddha, accomplishment to all people, benefit to the monastery, and merit to the devotees, because all this is a thousand years in one moment, and one moment in a thousand years.

LIKES AND DISLIKES

心甘情願

Everybody has one's own character. As a child, I was prone to sentiments of liking and disliking — just like everyone else. Tirelessly I would work day and night on things I enjoyed; with something I do not like doing, however, I would discard like a pair of worn-out shoes. One day my great-grandmaster, Master Cho Ch'ên, said to me, "Certainly you should do the things that you enjoy doing, but you ought also to possess restraint. For things that you do not like doing, if they should benefit others, you must similarly initiate resolution and do them." Since then, I started making every effort to do things that I might not always enjoy but would be beneficial to others.

Reciting Sutras and Prostrating for Repentance. Raising Monastic Sustenance

Ever since becoming a monk, I have never been very good at conducting major Dharma functions. But to give monastic members in distant areas a hand, I, cloaked by the stars, carrying the moon on my shoulder, and crossing ridge upon ridge of mountains, would often walk a hundred kilometers in one day just to make it to a Buddhist service. Having done this for several years, I knew not how many *yen-k'ou* (flaming mouth) ceremonies[1] I had attended. Thoroughly imbued with what I heard and saw on these occasions, I learned every kind of chanting and instrument-playing, and familiarized myself with the rituals of the Dharma functions. I grew to appreciate the Dharma joy that the equally egoistic and altruistic approaches of Buddhism could bring. However, with the state of affairs whereby most temples were anxious to conduct services, and delivering the dead was more important than delivering the living, I was never quite in agreement.

At twenty-two, I took up the post of director at Hua-ts'ang Temple in Nanjing. Despite a range of newly devised monastic regulations, I remained tolerant about the frequency of this type of services in order to keep in with the senior monks and for the long-term effect of improving upon some of the existing traditions. After coming to Taiwan, I vowed to engage myself in work oriented in culture and education. I would rather put up

[1] A ceremony in which Buddhist teachings are given and food is offered to beings in the realm of hell to relieve them from sufferings.

with hunger and poverty than waver even slightly in my principles. Thirty years ago, in establishing Shou-shan Buddhist College, I broke with my own rules to come up with funds. From dusk to dawn in the mortuary, I chanted sutras to deliver the dead. I felt neither put upon nor worn out because I was gathering monastic sustenance for the sake of the wisdom of all beings throughout the eons. As I saw the Buddhist colleges established one by one and graduating Buddhists by the thousands contributing spiritually and physically for the sake of Buddhism, I was deeply gladdened and consoled.

I have neither any music background nor much interest in such matters as joyous singing or lyrical recitation. However, to enable the proper faith of Buddhism to spread throughout Taiwan, I sought to inspire devotional enthusiasm by writing poems and lyrics myself and inviting others to compose the music. A Buddhist choir was formed and a choral instructor appointed. The choir traveled about raising their voices in song to welcome audiences. In such a way, the deep and abstruse Dharma was espoused and conveyed to the hearts of many by voices both light-hearted and gentle. I continued to organize contests and concerts, recorded albums, and distributed videos, all of which attained a wide appeal. As a person who is absolutely disinclined toward *do-re-me* and who has not an inkling of what musical scores stand for, I am living proof that, so long as one has the dedication, one can still turn music and song into the sound of the Dharma and let it flow far and wide.

Seven-day Pureland & Ch'an Retreats. All Wondrous Vehicles

Since starting to study Buddhism, I have always vowed, in my endless rebirths, to return and deliver all living beings. Much as I realize the blissful state of forgetting the self from reciting the Buddha's name, I have never taken rebirth in the Pureland as the goal of my religious practice. Nevertheless, when first preaching the Dharma in Taiwan, I not only set up groups to recite the Buddha's name in various locations but also conducted the seven-day Pureland retreat on a regular basis to expound the key points of reciting the Buddha's name. I had carried on like this for over thirty years. Many of the initial followers, on account of reciting the Buddha's name, took refuge in the Triple Gems; some became monastics while others came to establish Buddhist households of their own. All of them have made immeasurable contributions toward the burgeoning expansion of Buddhism in Taiwan. Reciting the Buddha's name and following religious practices not only adorn the Pureland of the next life but also purify the world of this life.

I had been trained in meditation halls at the Chin-shan and T'ien-ning Temples and elsewhere in the mainland. In seven-day Ch'an retreats, despite my own experience of the extreme joy of meditation, I do not advocate sitting in deep concentration like dead wood and still ashes. For the true essence of Ch'an originates in the mind, not in solitary and wearisome sitting. But to maximize public appeal, not only would I hold seven-day Ch'an retreats on numerous occasions, but also in other instances, such as short-term monastic retreats and summer camps for teachers and college students, classes in Ch'an meditation would be included. Fo Kuang Shan is in the middle of planning a large-scale meditation hall. By way of proper Ch'an practice and training of the mind, I hope to see the entire society hasten toward good fortune, amity, peace, and happiness.

Sutric and Tantric Traditions in Harmony

A Tantric rinpoche once told me that, to study his religion, a ten-year foundation in Sutric traditions is a prerequisite, or else it would be easy to fall into the pervert. When later I entered the secular world to propagate Buddhism, neither did I promote the practice of esoteric Buddhism, nor was I biased against it. Quite on the contrary, I had hosted the World Sutric and Tantric Buddhist Conference and Dharma functions in which the three practices of Ch'an, Pureland, and Tantric Buddhism were combined to urge understanding among all traditions and to unify the forces of Buddhism for the benefit of the world and emancipation of humankind.

I was a child from a poor family. On entering the monastic life to be educated, material goods were even more scarce. The daily three meals were often discontinued; I was never warm enough from the tattered old garments of fellow students and friends of the order. Such severe living conditions as these in the long run helped develop in me the habit of never purchasing on the street. But on a tour to Penghu or some other small islands to spread Buddhism, or a trip abroad to propagate the Dharma, I would not hesitate to loosen my purse strings for a souvenir or two from local vendors in order to cultivate friendship and bring joy to all. On my return I would be at a loss as to what to do with all those objects, but I would always enthuse in being generous as circumstances should dictate.

If Not Me, Who Then?

Ten years of character-building by way of rigid education in a large monastery enabled me not only to just smile at life's adversities but also to delight in complying with others. I relish neither isolation nor leadership. However, when I first arrived in Taiwan, I encountered oppression from senior monks on all fronts. I had no other alternative but to acknowledge the situation and seek self-fulfillment. Through the years I had repeatedly been ostracized by fellow monastics. Perhaps it was a case of our faiths not sharing the same origin, or it was simply because we were neither colleagues nor schoolmates. But, if a religion stands fragmented and lacks the mutual recognition of those within, how can it ever be united in a common endeavor?

With the gracious devotion and support

of followers toiling diligently these many years, we have brought Buddhism to the five continents. Honorary citizenships, symbolic keys, and even the honorary chair of World Fellowship of Buddhists, I have never asked for, but, when the request of the masses makes it hard to object to, I will accept with joy. In 1985, without the slightest attachment, I passed Fo Kuang Shan over to my disciples to oversee. In 1992, I organized Buddha's Light International Association in the hope that it might take the Buddha's light across the entire universe and bring fortune to humankind.

Stepping into Society with Compassion and on One's Vows

As a youth I studied at some of the oldest monasteries in remote mountains. I became accustomed to winds stirring pine leaves, water splashing river banks, birds singing, and insects sounding. I was used to sights of mountain streams in summer, valleys in autumn, flowers in spring, and snow in winter. Having grown up in nature's embrace, I do not like utilizing complicated, cold machinery. However, when finances became more abundant, I would buy recorders and cameras for the needy so that everyone might share in the joys of civilization. Television sets were transported from Hong Kong and distributed to relatives, old neighbors, and acquaintances in the mainland until excessive demands called for restraint on my part. My disciples, out of reverence for their master, would often bring me an electronic gadget or two. What a pity that, much accustomed to a simple life style and not liking to fiddle with buttons and keys, all I could do was to give these items away.

I am by nature an introvert; I do not like talking too much, and take pleasure in being quietly on my own to observe and ponder. But when I stepped into the murky mundane world to discover its need for the nourishment of Buddhism, I no longer remained quietly isolated but began to seek contact with the masses. My timid nature gave way to speaking about the sutras and the Dharma on stage and receiving followers when off. For years I have been in the company of the pubic daily, hold not the key to my own room, have not a single letter unreadable to others, and move not where others should not know. I have come to belong to the public. Although this means sacrificing time to myself, it is also in this way that the strength of my benevolence and vows are cultivated.

And so, despite having undergone

isolated practice, I do not necessarily feel that one must practice in such a manner; despite having maintained a diet of not eating after noon, I am not of the opinion that it is absolutely required. A real religious practitioner ought to be a Bodhisattva amongst the people. The welfare of society should always precede matters of personal clothing, eating, dwelling, and traveling. Better yet, I am not bound by my own conventions. Besides the construction of several fully equipped chambers for isolation, I would assist those in their retreats by visiting them and guiding them through any obstructions that they would encounter.

Meeting Guests from Afar. Following Circumstances Without Anguish

From a very young age, I had been accustomed to simple food and drink. Adding my lazy disposition to this, all three daily meals have always honored simplicity and convenience. Ordinarily, a bowl of tea-rice and one kind of vegetable would suffice to make me extremely content. But, whenever I go somewhere to spread the Dharma, followers always generously indulge me with the finest in food. Often before the first meal has been digested, the second feast is coming along. These occasions occurring without cease, I privately find them quite taxing at times. However, I would accept the hospitality, and do my best to contain my own discomfort if it means pleasing others. If asked what, in my entire life, I least enjoy doing, without any hesitation the answer would be: dinner parties, photograph sessions, and not being able to conveniently go to the bathroom when constantly caught among crowds — in that order. Nevertheless, upon seeing the pious joy of followers, I honestly cannot in any such scenario bring myself to be disagreeable.

Arrivals and departures on trips to propagate the Dharma are also a kind of tribulation. Always fearful of troubling others, I would like to come and go in silence. More often than not, situations do not abide by one's desires. Forty years ago, whenever I went south to Kaohsiung to lecture on the sutras, followers would invite a band to play all the way up the road and greet us at the train station in great fanfare. To avoid astonishing passersby, I switched to the evening train. Still undaunted, followers spared no pains to hasten to greet me and see me off. Until now, whether it be domestic, abroad, in the city, or in the countryside, the great kindness and hospitality of virtuous men and devout women remain on the increase. Sometimes they greet me in prostration, with fresh flowers and fruits, or ask the police or army to be a road escort. In July 1993, I went to Russia to found a chapter of Buddha's Light International Association. Carlos Liao, to my surprise, hired six secret police, who escorted me to St. Petersburg and back without once venturing even half a foot from my side. Seeing people so hard at work and busy on my behalf makes me feel very much in their debt. On the other hand, if I invariably refused them, it would not be entirely reasonable. What we consider our likes and dislikes, then, should accord with prevailing circumstances.

I have always been unskilled at calligraphy and never quite enjoyed being photographed. But upon seeing the faces of followers brighten with joy, I would always accede to their wishes. The only thing is, most of the time when I acquiesce to requests, I am unable to stop as I would like to. To write several dozen pieces of calligraphy a time is a common occurrence, and the waves of people wanting pictures come one after another. My legs would be aching and my feet numb, but I would persevere in complying and putting up with what they ask of me — I cannot think about what I like and dislike.

That Which One Ought to Do; That Which One Does Not Do

Witnessing in my youth the lawlessness of the warlords and recklessness of politicians filled my heart with great resentment. That was why I have never thought much of politics. Regardless, "the rise and fall of a country is the responsibility of every ordinary individual," not to mention the monastics. Holding on to the benevolence and compassionate vows of the Buddha, one ought to leave aside personal gain or loss and do what should be done for the good of all. Thus I recommended the opening of the door of democracy and advocated harmony between the two coasts. When circumstances ripened for the propagation of the Dharma, of those who came forward to listen to the sutras and ask about the Dharma, there was no shortage of military and political figures. I treated them with common courtesy and never overstepped the bounds of a monastic. Nonetheless, my name became involved in politics. Upon reflection, I keep a clear conscience, never quite letting things bother me. Furthermore, for a country and society to attain political harmony and peaceful joy via the Buddhist path would be a good thing indeed. Notwithstanding the fact that I have not the least intention to become active in politics, I will "go forward against thousands and tens of thousands," seek good fortune for all, and cast aside any notion of what I like and dislike as a person.

I still remember the faces of some fellow participants dimming with disapproval as soon as they saw me stand up to speak in past Buddhist conferences. They considered me to be a radical. But I am really quite conservative and obstinate about tradition. I had recommended that followers belong to the faith of Buddhism and religious property to the temples. I advocated that Buddhism be united under one common system, and hoped that national and civic ceremonies be patterned upon Buddhist standards. While researching the purpose behind monastic regulations implemented by ancient sages, I have never ceased to seek breakthroughs, renewals, and betterment in the Buddhist affairs. We should not confine ourselves to tradition, get into a rut, or be satisfied with present circumstances. The method of spreading the Dharma and teaching the sutras must continue to improve, and various approaches to give impetus to Buddhism worldwide be applied. For the future of Buddhism and the felicity of all beings, it is my feeling that, for all Buddhists, there ought only to be what they do and not do. About personal likes and dislikes, one need not be overly concerned.

Benefit of All Living Beings Before Own Gain or Loss

I dislike fame, but for twenty years I have accumulated quite some recognition. I dislike managing financial affairs, but for many construction projects I had to map out financial strategy and raise funds to meet the everchanging needs. I dislike haggling, but I cannot allow myself to become perfunctory in handling matters or let persistent vice gradually define my way. I dislike authority, but it is only proper that I preside over what is fair out of a sense of justice. In carrying out my grandmaster's directions I have done a lot of things that I do not really enjoy doing. But, with the passing of time, this is how I have led my life.

What is it, after all, that I truly like? I enthuse both in activity and serenity. It turns out that, however, personal causation and conditions have not accorded with this, and a few interests of mine are buried deep in my heart.

As a child I liked writing idly in my spare time of experiences and thoughts of all kinds. I had made a vow to spread the Dharma through the written word but, both unexpectedly and contrary to my wishes, the hectic itinerary which propagating the Dharma involves has made it impossible for me not to set aside this interest of mine. I have never taken it as a pity, for in losing something one must be gaining something else, and in gaining something one must be losing something else. The greatest satisfaction has come from seeing the joyous faces of followers listening to the Dharma. Are not the likes of Reverends Yi Kung and Yung Yun carrying on what I could have enjoyed doing myself? "It is not I who must be successful," and to this end, let me "initiate common practices without assuming leadership."

When I was only six or seven, I really liked to swim. I could be in the water for hours without sinking. Subsequently, the thing that I found hardest about being a monastic was severing my connection with water. Much as I like such sports as basketball, there were no classes in physical education when I was studying in the Buddhist college. Once I secretly made my own basketball hoop and rack, and ended up nearly dismissed. During those early years in Taiwan, people were generally conservative, so when I wanted to play basketball with students, to my surprise they would try to evade me. I felt extremely disappointed: as a student, my teacher would not let me play ball; as a teacher, my students would not dare play ball with me. What could I have done? I was close to fifty years of age before a basketball court was built atop Fo Kuang Shan. I could not have been happier! Everyday at dusk I would steal the ball from the novice monks, shoot the basket, and generally have a great time! The only problem in all this delight was that, usually at halfgame, I would hear my attendant call. Still perspiring, I had to throw on my robe before rushing over to the guest hall to meet with visitors. In recent years, busy as I have been lecturing both at home and overseas, often I would not even sit long enough to warm my seat. So I would put down the sport which I enjoy and continue politely in matters, some of which I do not enjoy quite as much.

A popular saying today is: "So long as I enjoy doing it, what is there that I cannot do?" This is precisely the root of social disorder. The

Buddha discovered more than 2,500 years ago the truth of dependent origination, the universe's mutual reliance. At the Hua-yen assembly,[2] he urged disciples to "pray that all beings be able to leave suffering and not seek individual ease and happiness." In all sincerity, happiness is what we are in pursuit of, but when all beings are still struggling and drowning in the dwelling of fire and the sea of suffering, how can we relentlessly succumb to relaxation, or even build our happiness upon others' suffering? All my life I have never really enjoyed my own interests; quite by contrast, I spend days toiling over many things that I do not quite like doing in the first place. Nonetheless, I live a life both full and rich, one which possesses the Dharma joy and natural ease, and which reaffirms for me the Buddhist outlook on life that is based on sacrifice and contribution.

What one likes is not necessarily good; what one dislikes is not necessarily bad. Living in this world, we sometimes have to sacrifice what we like, exchange interests for responsibilities, and do what are to be for the betterment of all.

[2] An assembly in which *Hua-yen ching (Avataṃsaka Sutra)* was expounded.

SPREADING THE
DHARMA TO BENEFIT
ALL SENTIENT BEINGS

While in my childhood, quite by chance I entered the monastic order, only to become the youngest student at Ch'i-hsia Vinaya College at the time. One day while reading, I came across a sentence which read: The sangha should view the spreading of the Dharma as its family obligation and the benefiting of all sentient beings as its career.

Young and inexperienced as I was, it was not until then that I realized that such is the sacred mission for us monastics to shoulder. I came to this instantaneous realization: I had waited too long to study Buddhism and engage in religious cultivation! Had I only been there a little earlier to cultivate and accumulate sagacity, I could have begun engaging in the work of the Buddha sooner. After this, each time I came across the line "pledging to serve the innumerable worlds with body and mind to repay the Buddha's grace" while reciting the *Mahāpratyangirā-dhāranī*, in my heart I made this vow: in the future I must contribute body and mind to spreading the Dharma and in benefiting all sentient beings.

To this day, I never tire of preaching, and my many Buddhist undertakings continue. In the blessings of the Buddha, nothing I have done in this life has not been for the sake of fulfilling this vow. True to say that "no vow will go in vain;" the hardship and suffering of the early years, however, were known to few.

In the 1950s, not only was life in Taiwan materially deprived, but it was like a desert wanting of the Buddhist Dharma. I resolved to sprinkle the sweet dew of the Dharma everywhere and reach out to the populace. With a group of resolute young people, we propagated the Dharma across the land in pioneering spirits. We left footprints all over the countryside, villages and towns, city streets and back alleys, temples and theaters, beaches and mountains. We wired electricity, fixed light bulbs, tuned microphones, laid out benches and stools, put up posters, and summoned audiences before taking the stage. For the few in number who came to listen, we were never downhearted, because if only one person would come, then one more person would be receiving the benefits of the Dharma. Often no one would show up at a lecture. I would start as usual, and it was after a long while that audiences gradually appeared. Later, people generally became punctual, and audiences became progressively larger. Sometimes people would start to move about, taking even their seats with them. When this happened, I would resort to a moment of silence, and it was not long before this counter-measure produced positive results!

Song of the Dharma Propagator Beneath the Zodiac and Among the Fields

To purchase equipment in the spread of Buddhism, I often exhausted all the donations. With one piece of bread to sate my appetite for the entire day was a common occurrence. To not too distant places, we would cycle. In pleasant weather, greeting the setting sun and basking in the evening wind provided a different kind of delight. But, when we ran into the early summer monsoons, wintry cold fronts, or days of typhoons, having to climb mountains or wade through water in desolate winds and insufferable rain was arduous indeed. Despite all this, to see the gradually growing audiences who also braved the wind and wet to come and listen to the Dharma was so moving it made me forget my own torment. En route to distant destinations by train, the pastoral sights were so fascinating that I became lost in their charm. Trains back then did not run very often, and many times we had to rush to the station after a Dharma function. Later on, station masters all along the Ilan line were so moved by the eager devotion we displayed that they would hold the trains until we had all boarded.

Most unforgettable to me is that each time we left at the end of a propagating function with devotees in escort, our hearts were filled with tender sentiments. We walked along paths in the fields and through forests and tunnels; we cut through the hush of the night singing in voices brimmed with the Dharma joy. Our hearts were as bright as the moon shining overhead, and our bodies felt as light as traces of wind that brushed them. Occasionally, we would exchange thoughts about spreading the Dharma. In discussing the work of Pūrna in converting and guiding the unruly masses, a sacrosanct sense of mission welled up among us; and discussing how Maudgalyāyana lost his life for Buddhism kindled a sense of tragic heroism. We swore to make high monks and virtuous men our models and furthering the existence of the Buddha's wisdom our purpose. One day, blessed with an inspiration, I set about to describe this outlook and mood in poetry. It was later put to music and became the song that we often sang aloud on the way back from spreading the Dharma, *Hung-fa chê chih ko* (Song of the Dharma Propagator).

Most consoling to me is that the young people who endured hunger and cold with us have matured through participation. Seeds that we all worked so hard to plant have blossomed into fruits of Bodhi. This is my life's richest harvest!

Through the years, as long as a place is in need of the Dharma or someone invites me, I would gladly abide no matter how far or how busy I am and even if I have to do without food or sleep. I remember one time on my way to Yuchih, a village in Nantu, to propagate the Dharma, we spent the night in a farmer's abode. As I slept on the floor next to the toilet, the stench was insufferable. There was no way I could get to sleep. In my desperate predicament, I had no alternative but to ask my travel companion, Venerable Chu Yün, to tell me stories. Later, in order to do justice to his diligent effort, I wrote *Yu Lin kuo-shih* (National Master Yu Lin) out of this story. Living in Ilan at the time, I often had to go to Kaohsiung to speak on the sutras. Each time I had to take the train and then change to the bus, a commuting complication which took an entire day. More often than not, I also had to economize on food and clothing so that I could scrimp enough together for the fare. Once when the ticket inspector came along checking tickets, I searched everywhere but could not find mine. Without a cent on me, I had no choice but to take out a new pen which I had not even begun to use and offer it in place of the missing ticket. I was constantly traveling between north and south like this for more than ten years, but it made me all the more joyous and tireless. Much more than the hardships of traveling, I fear that people do not know the benefits of the Buddhist Dharma. I have since traveled across Taiwan, as far away as the distant islands, and to varying international localities. People comment that I have far too much ambition wandering all over the world to propagate the Dharma when I am already retired! Such talk cannot be more off the mark! Although I have retired from the abbotship, I have not stopped being a monk. This is not an ambition but a vow.

Today, I no longer need to publicize my lectures; wherever I go, there is a willing audience. I used to worry that not enough people would show up to listen to me; now the overcrowded audiences are often a problem. I cannot bear to see people without tickets brave strong winds or the blazing sun to wait to enter the lecture hall. I cannot bear to see the lecture hall so crowded that there is not even room to stand. Most of all, I cannot bear having pious men and women kept outside because either the facility cannot accommodate them or they have arrived slightly late. Many times I asked those in charge to make exceptions, only to be ruled out by regulations. In 1992, I spoke at Dewan Tengku Abdul Rahman in Malaysia. The facility was filled to capacity, and more than a thousand did not have a seat. Outside were two more thousands who, unable to gain entry, pounded the doors and shouted, "Let us in! Our master having come this far, can't we take a look at him?" A few took to the fire escape or resorted to other unorthodox means to gain entrance. I will never forget how moved I was by such devotion.

In a Great Undertaking, Why Cherish One's Life!

Monastics concern themselves over spiritual cultivation, not poverty. The joy from the Dharma is enough to offset any material deficiency arising from their life styles. It is man-made obstructions that are the hardest tests for the propagation of the Dharma.

The first time I was to lecture on the sutras

in Ilan, I remember that the police prohibited me to speak publicly and to show slides. The reason was that I had not applied to the proper authorities! At a Dharma function in Lei-yin Temple, some heretical residents caused a ruckus outside. Also, at the last moment after the radio station had finished recording the lecture and the television station had finished producing their program, we encountered the misfortune of being canceled "due to the policy of the authorities in prohibiting the broadcast of religious programs." With hearts full of good will, we wanted to visit military bases and prisons to deliver the men and women from their suffering but were coldly refused. We asked: "Why are Roman Catholic priests and nuns and other Christian ministers able to go to these places to evangelize, while Buddhist monks are blocked outside the door?" They answered: "Because it's not proper for members of the monastic order to go in and speak on the Dharma." When we pressed them further, asking: "We're all religious figures spreading our faiths, but why are Buddhists treated differently?" What we got in reply was more indifference. Once when Taipei Normal College, now National Normal University, invited me to lecture and posters had already been displayed, the event was canceled the last moment for no reason. At other times when speaking publicly on the Dharma, the images of the Buddha which we used were subjected to discrimination. I never bemoaned these circumstances, or felt sorry for myself as a result of all this. Quite the contrary, frustration encourages me. For it is said, "In a great undertaking, why cherish one's life!"

In his practicing days, the Buddha had his body cut into pieces by Kalirāja. He blamed no one. I, in response to Kṣitigarbha Bodhisattva's "vowing not to become a Buddha until hell itself is empty," encourage myself by repeating: I will emulate the selfless spirit that all Buddhas and Bodhisattvas possess in serving the Dharma.

With unassuaged lament and resentment still lingering in my heart, I was further investigated by the public security authorities who had acted on some defamatory tips. I did not become cynical of the world because of this, but have learned to face the endless hindrances and slanders with a sense of the ordinary. I promise myself to strive without rest for the sake of Buddhism's eternal mission; I want to work without slack for the sake of the life of wisdom of the uncounted sentient beings. My unfaltering ideals have produced positive yields. I have come to be invited to speak on the Dharma for police and military institutions alike. Many finely constructed and renovated temples are attributed to years of spreading the Dharma. I work regularly with the media to broadcast on the Dharma. In every public appearance, I have been treated with utmost courtesy and cooperation.

The biggest problem I have had to face in propagating the Dharma is how to appropriately adjust to the aptitude of the audience. In the beginning, I would spend long hours trying to guess the mind-set of the audience for the sake of preparing a single speech. Moreover, I would ponder over the deeper significance of a term again and again in the hope that everybody might, first, be able to understand and benefit from it, and, second, be able to utilize the marvelous truth of the Dharma as a compass for the practical way of life.

Never pedantic or abstruse, I have always been of a single mind and purpose, and propagate the Dharma as a cross-reference in everyday life. Contemplating Buddhism's modernity and farsightedness, I hope to pass on generations of wisdom and achievements to our descendants, thereby carrying on from the past while opening the way for the future.

To meet the needs of devotees and allow the Dharma to reach all levels of society, I seek to organize chanting groups, youth choirs, sunday schools, Dharma seminars, art programs, and even float parades on the Buddha's birthday. These efforts have drawn the censure and condemnation of many conservatives. But I would not be held back. As long as Buddhism could thrive because of my efforts, why should I be concerned over personal fortune or misfortune?

Turning Exhaustion into the Strength of Vows

My perseverance has resulted in the wide acceptance of a humanitarian Buddhism, a kind of living Buddhism. Activities at temples and monasteries constantly generate a potent force of devotees. Many young people who studied Buddhism with me have taken up their positions as administrators in Fo Kuang Shan.

That I started out as one serious thinker but have ended up with a more thorough grasp and penetrating insight of Buddhism than expected is to me such a harvest. I go among the masses to learn to inculcate according to individual aptitude. Soldiers and farmers, laborers and businessmen, the old and the infirm, women and children, widows and widowers, and orphans and the lonely are all my target audience. Today, my daily itinerary is filled with invitations to propagate the Dharma. Always on the go, I hardly sit long enough — it seems — to warm a seat; other times, I wake up not knowing where I am. But, what is this little effort on my part compared to the Buddha who, at the age of eighty, traveled on foot throughout India preaching the Dharma without uttering so much as a word about hardships? At the sight of many nodding their heads in realization, clapping, and laughing, my fatigue turns into an incomparable force of conviction. Upon seeing so many find refuge in the Triple Gems, I rejoice, knowing that they have begun new lives for themselves.

Once on a train, a youth I did not know offered his seat to me. He said quietly, "Master, I am a devotee of yours who took refuge in the Buddha when you held a Dharma function at a penitentiary!" No other courteous treatments in the past would be etched more deeply in my memory than this particular incident. I have received numberless notes of thanks from people who have come to mend their wrongful ways and return to virtue, couples and friends who are reconciling, failed examinees who find new hope, unemployed youths who once again are forging ahead, and suicidal people who are prepared to go back on track. I have received many verses of praise, some of which are not exactly fluent and articulate, but the sincerity always moves me so! The souvenirs that I have received are so plentiful that, rather than warehousing them, I rejoice in redistributing them.

Spreading the Dharma as Family Obligation. Benefiting All Sentient Beings as Career

I find happiness not only in speaking on the Dharma, but also in the promotion of learning and the cultivation of future propagators. During the span of a forty-year career in delivering the masses, donations are always given first to building lecture halls and classrooms, and fees from writing I have used in the purchase of reference books for students. In the early days of Fo Kuang Shan, devotees had urged me to buy a car for myself. Instead, a bus was bought for the benefit of everybody. Beginning recently, I have been transferring publishing royalties to cover personal expenses and transportation costs in order that the burden on the monastery be reduced.

For thousands of years, the written *prajñā* has facilitated Buddhism being transmitted across the world. Having recognized this, when I first came to Taiwan I promptly applied my energies in cultural undertakings such as writing articles, editing magazines, and publishing books. In 1959, a center for Buddhist cultural service was set up in Sanchungpu to print Buddhist sutras. The extremely dire financial conditions and serious shortage of editing and printing staff were supported on sheer devotion to deliver all beings, which saw me through those days of distress. I would stay up the whole night editing and then take the manuscript to press, not realizing I had gone without food for the entire day. I got into the practice of reusing the back of papers other people had thrown away for my modest works. To this day, I continue cultural undertakings such as putting out magazines and books despite yearly losses. For I am fully aware of one thing: no living being is too far away to be reached by the power of the Buddhist culture. This is something not to be emulated by material wealth.

The founding of free clinics, retirement homes, kindergartens, winter relief camps, and other relief ventures had spread the Buddhist kindness to the aged, infirm, handicapped, poor, and suffering. The founding of Fo Kuang Shan has initiated a burgeoning economic development around. After all, the monastery is, in itself, an enormous enterprise geared toward benefiting and relieving all living beings both near and far. Haven't Buddhist monasteries and temples always contributed to both state and social well-being?

The sight of a vacant plot would immediately make me think of building a monastery or a lecture hall; the sight of an acquaintance would set me working to include him or her in the Buddhist fold; the sight of something good happening would give me cause to proclaim it far and wide. I want but to be able to disseminate the joy of Buddhism to all living beings.

People used to say this about me: "What a pity! So young, and already a monastic." I could not disagree more. What pity is there in renouncing the mundane life, becoming a monastic, and spreading the Dharma for the benefit of all living beings? Not only is it an honor to be a monastic here in this life, but also will I make this vow: in all my future lives I want to follow the Buddha's spirit of teaching, advising, benefiting, and rejoicing, and I want to come to this *sahā* world[1] as a monk who views spreading the Dharma as his family obligation and the benefiting of all sentient beings as his career.

[1] The world of bearing of sufferings.

BUDDHISM
DEPENDS ON ME

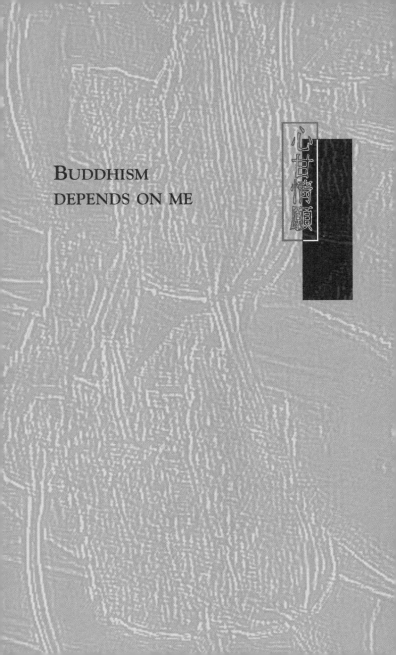

I first arrived in Taiwan in 1949. At the time, war in mainland China had caused widespread panic, and many monastics were fleeing the country. One day, Venerable Chu Yün brought me a letter from Venerable Ch'ên K'ung, who was practicing in solitude at P'u-t'o Shan.

Venerable Ch'ên K'ung, an eminent disciple of Venerable Master T'ai Hsü, had earlier worked as an editor for *Hai-ch'ao yin* (Sounds of the Tidal Wave), a monthly Buddhist magazine. I was fortunate to have had the opportunity to be acquainted with him when I was receiving training at Chiao Shan, and I deeply respected his manner as an elder and his compassion for his students. I was particularly happy to hear from him. During the war, a letter from a friend was worth a million gold pieces, and I could hardly wait to open it. His letter read:

> The young sangha of today should have the conviction that Buddhism depends on them rather than that they depend on Buddhism.

It Takes One to Preach the Dharma. The Dharma Does Not Preach Itself

As I read the letter, its advice shook me deeply. In chaos, no one knew what the next moment would hold. Ignorance and lack of faith in the Buddhist teachings had led many devotees in Taiwan to pursue paths of superstition, burning incense and praying for mundane blessings. So degraded, it was small wonder that Buddhism was not high in the society's regard.

Within the Buddhist circle, the confidence of young monks and nuns was also shaken. Temples would not accept monastics other than their own; novices had no chance to consult with elders; writings were not allowed to be published; and opportunities to preach the Dharma were restricted. All in all, it was impossible to rely on the Buddhist community for survival.

I was pushed to the brink of despair. Then, the words of Venerable Ch'ên K'ung returned to mind, working on me like a stimulant and strengthening my confidence and faith: "It takes a person to preach the Dharma; the Dharma does not preach itself." How true! We must understand that the existence of Buddhism lies in our hands, and that we must accept the responsibility for its continuance. These thoughts I kept engraved deeply in my mind, and I shared them with my Dharma brothers in mutual encouragement.

That same year I traveled from Taichung to Taipei. Within a short interval of two days, the following happened to me. At a temple on Nan-chang Road, a master demanded of me: "What qualifies you to stay in Taiwan?" I went on to a temple on Chung-cheng Road and was again rejected. The night was cold and rainy. The only place to rest was under a large bell, where I slept in my soaked clothing.

Another time, I arrived at a temple in Keelung at one in the afternoon in the hope of getting some lunch, which I had missed the day before, only to find that the temple was ordered not to give food to traveling monks.

Yet another time, I had hoped to stay at Cheng-tzu Liao on Kuan-yin Shan. But on my way there I discovered that the road was flooded. Stuck at a bus stop, I peered into the gusty wind and pouring rain, cold and hungry. I wondered where else to go.

Thoughts of the misty skies over Taipei or the rugged and torturous mountain paths of Keelung are still so ineffable! That I was able to live through those difficult times was because of my faith in Buddhism. The inconveniences imposed on me I took as tests of faith and endurance. After all, what are personal hardships compared with those of the Buddha!

It was no easy task looking for a temple to accept me, but I finally found one. In gratitude I offered to do all the menial jobs. I went for groceries early each morning, cleaned the bathrooms, and drew six hundred pails of well water for the temple's daily consumption. When I had a free moment, I would tend the garden, look after the old and decrepit, take care of the cremations, guard the forest at Tahu, and cook and serve everyone at mealtime. I was not being very useful really, but I was inspired by the thought that the existence of Buddhism rests in my hands. I must be accepted by others before I would have an opportunity to contribute to Buddhism and serve all beings.

As time went on, I was offered more positions. Venerable Miao Kuo asked me to be abbot of Fa-yün Temple. Venerable Wu Shang wanted me to manage Ling-yin Temple. Venerable Tz'ŭ Hang recommended me to preach at T'ien-lung Temple. Sung Hsiu-chên encouraged me to study at Tê-lin Library. These propositions demonstrated that the

Buddhist faith is warm and hearty, and competent people are cherished. To begin, let Buddhism depend on us rather than us on Buddhism.

Strength and Endurance by a Hundredfold

From 1949 through 1952, with little recognition I did what I could for Buddhism from a sense of responsibility that was solely mine. I criticized the plot of *Huo-shao hung-lien ssǔ* (Burning of Red Lotus Temple) because it slandered Buddhism. I argued against Chu Shih-ying's proposal to change the objectives of *Chüeh-ch'ün* (Awakening the Masses). When the government wanted to prohibit religious rites, I proposed a reform instead. I helped raise funds for earthquake victims in Hualian, mailed Buddhist literature to the front lines in the Korean War, opposed the Legislative Counsel's permitting Spanish bullfights in Taiwan, and confronted the police numerous times for the freedom to preach the Dharma.

It was not easy practicing the words "Buddhism depends on me." One must have the ability and strength to withstand the adversity. I recall a time when some individuals convinced a Shanghai opera company to ostracize me from their Taipei stage production of *Yu Lin kuo-shih* (National Master Yu Lin), a story I had written. The Central Broadcasting Station was asked not to let me write the script. Another time Taipei Normal College, now National Normal University, invited me to lecture, but someone had the invitation canceled even after posters were put up. When Venerable Lcan-skya gegen nominated me to represent Chinese Buddhist Association in the World Fellowship of Buddhists conference in Nepal, yet someone else made sure that did not happen. These experiences were but so trivial, as I had confidence to make it through each and every.

Later, with my disciples I produced a radio program called *Fo-chiao chih shêng* (The Buddhist Voice), which aired for six years, and hosted Buddhist programs for more than ten years at all three television stations in Taiwan. Lecture engagements with colleges and schools are more than I can handle. But I have never really belonged to any group. Today, Buddha's Light International Association, established in May 1992, shines all over the world.

We must not fear defeat; only we can defeat ourselves. As I reminisce on the hardships of the last forty years, no words can do them justice. But in the words of Venerable Ch'ên K'ung, I got by indeed with the conviction that Buddhism depends on me rather than that I depend on Buddhism.

THE RAREST OF ENCOUNTERS

心甘情願

My life can be characterized by many different beliefs and notions that I reflect upon repeatedly. Amongst them, the consideration of that which is truly the rarest of encounters has benefited me immeasurably all life long!

That I was born in the historically renowned Yangchou, Chiangsu province was what I feel to be the rarest of encounters. My father was loyal, prudent, and rich in experience, and my mother, bright and capable. That in my childhood I was treated by my parents both with love's sustenance and a strict discipline was to me the rarest of encounters. Later, through a very natural unfolding of events, Venerable Master Chih K'ai was requested to give me the tonsure. Manifesting a great capacity for magnanimity, Master Chih K'ai did not want to see me end up waiting upon him for the rest of my life, and so he soon delivered me into the service of the masses of all directions. That is, I was entered into a large monastery where I was to undergo rigorous religious training for the good of humankind. Being fit to study under such a great master was to me truly the rarest of encounters.

I became a monastic at Ch'i-hsia Shan, also known as "the capital of six dynasties and the famous monastery of one thousand Buddhas." In an ancient monastery deep in the mountains, for ten years I witnessed not only peaches and apricots blossom under the warmth of spring but also maple leaves blanketing the mountain slopes in the depths of autumn. On my way to attaining the body of the Dharma and life of wisdom, I not only underwent the severe and authoritative tests of my spiritual peers, but also got a taste of the harsh discipline of an uncompromising monastic education. Through this transformation, I could not have been more appreciative of it all being the rarest of encounters. When later my wanderings in search of Buddhist teaching took me as far away as Taiwan, I first settled in a monastery, where I carried firewood, hauled water, pulled carts, made purchases, and patrolled the mountainscape night and day. Not a single one of these rare and precious experiences did not play some part in building my fortitude or nourishing my conviction in the years that followed.

Through Good Fortune and Bad

My introspective nature drove me to join a circle of individuals closely tied to Buddhist cultural activities at the time I first came to Taiwan. But editorial work left me in the lurch, often not having enough to eat or a place to stay. I became involved with Buddhist education, but before long, activities at the Buddhist college were suspended. Rendered unable to do anything else, I was then forced to pluck up my courage and enter the society at large as a propagator of the Dharma. Indeed, it was under such circumstances that I began coming in contact with the public on a much broader scale. At the same time I began "cultivating a perspective on existence which equates the self with the masses." One might remark what rare and precious encounters this string of events appears.

I cannot recall the times I was invited to speak on the sutras and spread the Dharma abroad between the ages of twenty-five and thirty. Unfortunately, not knowing English, I had no choice but to reluctantly decline the kind offers. Many monasteries had asked me to preside over their Dharma functions, but, Buddhist chanting and recitation not being my strengths, I had to turn these warm gestures down. In hindsight, it was precisely because of this that I became settled on the spreading of the Dharma for the welfare of all beings as my sole mission in life. How can this not be said to reflect the rarest and most precious set of circumstances! In the early years the mentality of the monastic circle in Taiwan was characterized by a conservatism which made Buddhism simply unattractive to the young. As such, to cultivate young Buddhists, the only route to follow was to build a new and independent temple. It was upon this ideal that Fo Kuang Shan was built. There is a passage which goes: "Facing the edge of the mountains, approaching the end of the river, this seems the end of the road; in the shade of the willows, through the light of the flowers — there, another village appears!" Every variation of hardship and obstacle, and any degree of paucity and want are but the rarest of encounters in the journey through adversity.

When I retired from the abbotship of Fo Kuang Shan in 1985, I was deeply thankful for the devotion that followers showed in not forgetting all about me. If I am not invited to lecture on the canon at one place, then I am asked to spread the Dharma somewhere else. Under a barrage of warm sentiments that is difficult not to yield to, I find myself left with little free time. In the process I seem to always be getting busier and busier, forever bustling about. But as my travels enable me to widen my sphere of affinity with others, that charge of Dharma joy brought about by those rarest of encounters always inspires and encourages my diligence. The founding of Buddha's Light International Association in 1992 and its steady expansion, in particular, represent a precious moment in the vast expanse of endless kalpas, the rarest of encounters indeed.

The benevolent concern and unselfish cooperation that others show me, be it the slightest gesture of kindness, I will forever regard as the rarest of good karma. Forty years ago spreading the Dharma in Ilan, my manuscripts were written atop a worn-out sewing machine until devotees brought me a discarded desk from a nearby jail. Such modest offerings, in line with gems and jewels, are the rarest of the rare for being from a sincere heart.

In my youth, for years I did not see three full meals in a day. An old woman, Ah-ch'ou Gu, would often bring over a bowl of noodles and two slices of bread to curb my hunger. Searching my conscience in the still of the night, I wondered what I did to deserve her great kindness when we were bonded but by a chance meeting. The loving charity reflected in the way she treated me both like a Buddhist master and a son was to me truly the rarest of encounters. In another instance, Mrs. Wang-Cheng Fa-lien and I did not really know each other well. But out of Buddhist piety, she took my two published works, *Wu shêng-hsi tê ko-ch'ang* (Singing in Silence) and *Yu Lin kuo-shih* (National Master Yu Lin), and quite unbelievably managed to sell two thousand copies of each by peddling them door to door. In a society where compassion sometimes seems to be about as thin as a sheet of paper, I am especially gratified by such rarest of encounters. Today the ninety-year-old Mrs. Wang resides at Fo Kuang Retirement Home, so that I am able to nourish and care for her during her twilight years.

In the last twenty or thirty years, not a few young disciples have followed me into the monastic order. In the spirit of "teaching to one and all," I have at present with me upwards of one thousand monastics. There are many more laypersons who uphold the Dharma and serve the principles of humanitarian Buddhism by supporting the construction of monasteries, contributing to the printing of Buddhist texts, helping out in any position and all situations where they are needed, and expending not only money but also effort. Such rarest of the rare encounters constantly renders me in awe.

Thankfulness be unto All Circumstances

Like the spring breeze and autumn shower invigorate all earthly creatures, the autumn frost and winter snow bring about the ripening of every life form. In my youth, my seniors used to beat and scold me ruthlessly and demand unreasonably of me. This had come to foster obedience in me, and instilled in me a perseverance which enabled me to journey through turbulent times. The early training was to me the rarest of encounters indeed.

When I first went on the road to preach the Dharma, I would often spend hours trying to churn out a good script or some illustrative material. But today, rushing from one engagement to the next, or speaking on the Dharma on formal occasions or whenever it is called for, I realize the Dharma is everywhere. The benevolent masses, willing as they are to listen to me, prompt me to study the Buddhist canon in depth, to comprehend the implicit wisdom therein, and to undertake religious practice. Each time I think of all this, only the words "the rarest of encounters" would suffice to convey the tremendous appreciation that I feel.

When cheated, I tell myself that being a monastic I must be magnanimous; when slandered, I think that being a monastic I must never be vengeful; and when harmed, I determine that being a monastic I must respond with kindness. After so long, no trying environment is yet to knock me off my stride. I only wish, for all beings, fortune, prosperity, longevity, and joy. There are times when people cause trouble for no reason whatsoever, but I am never exasperated. I pray that the wisdom of all sentient beings in the dharma realm be vast like the ocean. For it is crucial, through the faith in the rarest of encounters, that those who owe a debt of karma, and those who have known glory and insult, and experienced slander and praise should become patient and tolerant, and be able to welcome adversity with a smile and feel at ease in it.

As I am able to view everything in the light of the rarest of encounters, all the good and bad, glorious and dismal in life have come to fill my days with happiness and fortune.

ONLY WEALTH WELL
SPENT IS REALLY
YOURS TO KEEP

心甘情願

Ｆrom 1952 I started to edit *Jên-shêng yüeh-k'an* (Life Monthly), a job which continued for six years in total. Once I heard Venerable Tung Ch'u, the publisher, utter this line: "Only wealth well spent is really yours to keep!" I have come to benefit endlessly from these words ever since.

I was born and raised in the shadow of poverty. Never with much means, I developed a habit of not buying or hoarding things. Such a habit not only helped me greatly through life but also led to a lifetime of Buddhist undertakings. For it is because I have no wealth that I accumulate none. Rather, I have come to discover the knack of wise spending. Indeed, possession of wealth, earned by past good deeds, is good karma. But the ability to spend well is true wisdom.

To Have Wealth is Good Karma. To Spend Well is Wisdom

In 1951, I became dean of studies of a Taiwan Buddhist training program and was on the pay-roll of the Taiwan Buddhist Association. The monthly salary, to any average person, would truly be the most paltry of paltry amounts. But for my monastic upbringing, which trained me not to be greedy or possessive of material objects, I felt that was a lot. Each month after I used the money to equip classrooms and school grounds and to purchase stationeries for the destitute students, hardly much was left. But to see the young progressing in Buddhist studies and eventually coming to be of use to the religious community filled me with much relief and joy. Are these students not, in a sense, the most invaluable wealth? For indeed, only wealth well spent will really be yours to keep.

Two years later, I found myself with the Buddhist chanting group in Ilan, earning a larger salary. It made me feel quite wealthy! Back then Protestantism was a popular faith in Taiwan; acknowledging this fact, an interesting idea came to mind. I spent half my income on a bunch of silver necklaces with *sauvastika*[1] pendants. I asked the young Buddhist devotees, who had been listening intently to the sutras and showing a strong inquisitiveness toward the Dharma, that they wear the necklaces as a symbol of noble religious identity. The purpose of this feat was .

[1] An auspicious sign of great antiquity and an emblem of Buddhism.

to let people know that, besides those who reverently wear a necklace with a cross pendant, there are as well those who feel it an honor to don a Buddhist pendant. With the other half of my monthly income I subscribed to one hundred copies of the Buddhist magazine *Jên-shêng* to provide devotees with good reading material. By 1954, with quite a raise I sent Chang Yu-li (Tzu Hui), Wu Suh-jen (Tzu Jung), and others to teachers' training for preschoolers. Reverend Yen Tzu and others, too, were enabled to study at Hsi Tze Buddhist College. In the end, those who read *Jên-shêng yüeh-k'an* joined me in the spreading of Buddhism, and those who trained in preschool education returned to either run the Buddhist kindergarten or serve in the monasteries and temples in other ways. For myself, I gained from these experiences an even deeper understanding of what it means by only wealth well spent is really yours to keep.

Spending on Education

In 1956, I turned down an opportunity to enter a doctorate program at Tai Sho University in Japan and channeled what would have been my tuition to a Buddhist cultural center and a reading program. Later, I was able to send Reverends Tzu Chuang, Tzu Hui, Tzu Jung, Tzu Chia, Tzu Yi, and others to study in Japan. At a time when Taiwan's economy was at its very worst, many laughed at me for being a fool with financial matters. But the way things turned out far exceeded any form of silver-tongued debate. All the monastics, on completion of their studies, returned to put to use what they had learned. In the last few decades, many young Buddhists were sent to pursue their studies, some even abroad. One after the other they returned to take their position at Fo Kuang Shan, proving time and again that only wealth well spent is really yours to keep.

In the average household with three to five children, the cost of schooling is already quite a burden. Even more considerable is how, for the thousand or so who followed me into monasticism, six Buddhist colleges were founded. Moreover, for the broadening of their world view, they were urged to learn through traveling. It all required untold sums every year. But I had never complained about being poor or in any way hard-pressed. For if one does not seed the fields, there will never be any harvest. Having wealth but not using it makes it far from being yours, no matter how you let it pile up.

Only wealth well spent is really yours to keep — especially when it is expended on cultivating people. To this end, I have never been the slightest stingy. However, when it comes to allotting funds, the hardest thing is to be exactly fair. I remember how in the early years that the youths who followed me into monasticism came from backgrounds both poor and affluent. In light of the fact that none of the young monastics had exactly the same needs, I decided to place all the funds where they could draw as much as they felt was necessary for them. I felt that to be true equality.

Remembering as far back as 1953, the spreading of Buddhism was invariably an outdoor event. Anything from installing a temporary light cost, hiring somebody to bang on a gong to spread the word, printing leaflets, to transportation would involve a cost. To have to cover these expenditures was extremely challenging. Though mired in financial instability, I continued to travel on limited funds to widen the influence of the Dharma. I constantly had to tighten my belt as I carried on without the benefit of even a basic diet. I also came up with funds to pay for radio broadcasts and was the first to buy air time on television, allowing the voice of the Dharma to be heard everywhere. The years passed by like a day. Isn't the prevalence of the Dharma today the natural blooming of Bodhi seeds scattered in the past? Let us not be afraid to expend wealth, because only wealth well spent is really yours to keep.

When editing *Jên-shêng yüeh-k'an*, I vigorously argued in the interest of greater readership appeal that the extent be increased from twenty pages to a total of twenty-eight, and promised to subsidize the extra cost regardless of the fact that I was without funds for such an expansion. During the days that followed, I lived more frugally than ever, scrimping down on food just so that I could come up with the payments to which I had committed myself. To be honest, spending was the least of my worries. As the only person editing and proofreading the magazine, there was no alternative for me but to work around the clock and cudgel my brain. But the added pages turned out to be a garden for my own literary creations. Both *Shih-chia-mou-ni Fo ch'uan* (Biography of Sakyamuni Buddha) and *Yu Lin kuo-shih* (National Master Yu Lin) were written during that period. As time passed, my own writing skills came to be more polished. Indeed, in Buddhism, giving is directed toward others, but it is also every bit giving to oneself. If I had been frugal and unwilling to finance the added pages, I would not have been able to cultivate in the process my own perception or ability to utilize my mind. Thinking about it now, only wealth well spent is yours to keep.

A Wealth of Wisdom from Not Coveting or Hoarding

Having gotten into the habit of writing, I energetically contributed articles to books, newspapers, and magazines alike. Each time I made a bit of money I would buy small gifts for devotees. I was not trying to give small favors, as I was not hoping for anything in return. All I had in mind was to build bonds of affinity. Many were thus encouraged to come and study the Dharma. The merchant who sold me the gifts made a small fortune. The business also brought him a sense of moral cultivation and a feeling that he was being protected by the Buddha. This fellow went on to seek refuge in the Triple Gems. Later, all over Taiwan gift shops selling Buddhist souvenirs sprang up. None of these could I ever have predicted. Indeed, only wealth well spent is really yours to keep.

For all the Buddhist books and periodicals I sent devotees as tokens of friendship, I would hope that their mind and the Dharma might merge into one purifying current to cleanse the world. As expected, many of the young people who had received my presents years ago now take the podium to speak on the Dharma. That such a small wealth could produce such rich harvests for Buddhism left an indelible impression on me. Truly, spending should not only be on personal needs; better still, it should be for the purchase of wisdom, a contribution to the masses.

I still remember how twenty-six years ago, I would always pay extra for the monastic's shoes that Yeh Peng-sheng's father made, or for a bowl of vegetarian plain noodles at the small noodle shop in Changhua which I frequented. Those who were with me questioned the rationale of all this. But I thought it perfectly reasonable. At a time when Buddhism was not at all common, I was making every small effort to encourage business ventures related to Buddhism. In a way I was hoping to "give away a brick and get a gem in return" so that not only could business people gain a little good fortune through Buddhism, but also followers could conveniently purchase Buddhist goods and people dine vegetarian.

Some cab-drivers in Hong Kong used to refuse to take monastics. Hoping to change this attitude, I would pay double of what the fare meter read. Later on, I did the same with peddlers and other business people. On my way to Penghu to lecture, I used to buy those little pebbles peddled by the locals. Upon returning, however, I never knew exactly what to do with them. Once in northern Thailand to spread the Dharma, I found myself pacing back and forth among the vendors' stalls for a very long while and looking desperately left and right to find something that I fancied. Trying to come up with an idea to remedy the situation, I, in the end, gave every vendor in the area a small sum as a gesture of charity — much to the wide-eyed astonishment of a hundred or so of them.

While on tour to scenic spots overseas, I would always take the lead in the purchase of souvenirs. Sure, I treat myself with the utmost frugality and do not really need any such souvenirs for myself. But, upon seeing me make a purchase, devotees in my company would do the same. Prompting devotees to join in a bond of affinity with the vendors would be a good thing indeed. Any devotee seen haggling with local merchants would be chided.

I make no habit of buying. But when the time comes that I must make a purchase, I will not go for a bargain for fear of causing others to lose money. Making purchases with a heart for cheery bonds of affinity would enable merchants to profit more and thus improve their products. Buying convenience for oneself is nothing like buying common good for all. For indeed, only wealth well spent is really yours and everybody else's to keep.

As early as 1965 when Shou-shan Buddhist College was founded, free food and accommodation were provided for the young people studying there. To maintain such a huge expenditure I had to be frugal in every possible way. Even though the ritualistic side of Buddhism was never my forte, I recited the sutras in funerals to raise funds. Receipt of any lucky money would promptly lead to the purchase of new equipments — on one occasion, a bench or two, and another time, a few books for the library. Slowly, classrooms grew in number and libraries were filled. I never considered this to be a burden, because right along purchases were made not just for the self but for all. Indeed, that only wealth well spent is really yours to keep is but an extension of equating the self with all, which I have practiced through the years.

Twenty years ago, when the clearing had just started on Fo Kuang Shan, I also donated a large sum to help Buddhist Compassion Relief Tzu Chi Foundation get on its feet. About the same time, I heard of a young man living in Taichung who wanted to pursue a doctorate in Buddhist studies in Japan but was hard up financially. Not having ever met him before, I delivered the funds to his home in person. Today, seeing the foundation flourish as it does and young scholars account so well for themselves in the Buddhist academia pleases me a great deal. So long as we manage our finance by the concept of "enjoying rather than possessing," then quite naturally we will be able to share in the happiness implicit to wealth which is well spent, and hence which is yours to keep.

Between Clean Wealth and Filthy Riches

In 1950, when Venerable Chu Yün withdrew to Taiwan from Chou Shan, I presented him with a newly tailored long robe. After this, through all of two years at Yuan-kuang Monastery, I wore only my short garment. Once in the traumatic early years of Fo Kuang Shan, a certain monastic asked to borrow a huge sum from me. Out of respect for his seniority, I did all I could to get the money together, only to discover the whole episode was meant to test my character. It left me with a bad taste indeed. On numerous trips to Japan, monastics would request their travel expenses be paid. In those days I had enough problem footing my own bill, let alone worrying about others'. I nonetheless made sure these needs be met. In the past, fellow monastics unwilling to stay and assist me, down and out writers, and those who inadvertently lost money all touched my compassion. I am not wealthy, but I am willing to share my wealth; nor have I ever become impoverished because of it. In expending wealth, as long as everybody is satisfied, I am satisfied also. What more is there to ask for? The only people I would be unwilling to help were the brazen-faced with a lion's mouth who asked amounts in the tens of thousands. For wealth, clean as it were, should not be allowed to become filthy riches.

While traveling far and wide to spread the Dharma, I would keep an open eye for any worthwhile Buddhist cultural relics. In the early days of poverty and hardship, I would skip a meal or two to make a purchase, or walk endless distances lugging some Buddhist statue to save on transportation. It all came to a point where I would be mocked by some fellow monastics, who thought I was running some smuggling deal. Not once did I bother to explain myself. A Buddhist cultural museum was built at Fo Kuang Shan in 1983, and an exhibition hall at Hsi Lai Temple, in 1988. Lately I am gathering Dharma relics for the vihara in an old castle in Paris. Every single piece of relic was acquired through years of painstaking effort. The enormous expense of maintenance often made it impossible to make ends meet. But endorsement from the many admiring visitors never fails to affirm my creed that only wealth well spent is really yours to keep. The cold and frigid relics contain in essence a copious life force. Without uttering a word, they proclaim the time-honored history and culture of Buddhism.

Thirty-five years ago, an impoverished young woman came to me, expressing her desire to study Buddhism with me. At the time I had difficulty finding a place to stay myself and was compelled to turn her down. Just as she was about to leave, I emptied what was in my pocket and gave her all as a gift, hoping she could seek out a Buddhist school and use the meager sum to cover expenses. Never would I have vaguely anticipated that, thirty-five years later, she would already have repaid me a hundred thousand times through her donations and in her efforts to preserve the Dharma and the sangha. She is none other than Huang Li-ming, known to many as Fairy Maiden Huang. When the opportunity presents itself, she still enjoys talking about how she entered the fold at Fo Kuang Shan. As for me, I have come to be more assured than ever that wealth well spent is not only yours to keep but will also bring about interest by a hundred thousand times! In giving away wealth, one is not to trade for a mere name or to dwell on the sheer amount but rather, as a result of giving in earnest, to win happiness and peace of mind.

I often make it a point to be there for disciples and monastics in times of difficulties. Among the various departments at Fo Kuang Shan, there are times when jurisdictional responsibilities, financial restrictions, or conflicting viewpoints lead to contention for funding. "Leave the money to me," I would say. At that, spears and shields of strife are replaced with jades and silks of harmony.

Years of peace at Fo Kuang Shan are indeed a personal harvest of mine. As always, I have maintained that only wealth well spent is really yours to keep.

Indeed, myself thus convicted and disinclined toward the stockpiling of wealth, and Fo Kuang Shan upholding the spirit of "means coming from all directions will go in all directions, together completing tasks in all directions," in the many years gone by not only was there never any surplus, but also the pressures of finance continue to be unrelenting. Not a day passes without its share of hardship, but each and every day does pass just the same — uneventful and serene. Nobody clamors to gain the abbotship or struggles to take the financial helm. Far from it. As we serve society and contribute to the populace in self-sacrifice, I would count my blessings — many times as meaningful as the mere possession of wealth.

Wealth Must Flow to be of Great Use

Looking on the world of billowing clouds of dust, some people are seen to just sit idle with their riches and valuables, but once dead, even before the corpse is cold, the children and grandchildren turn to bicker nonstop over the distribution of assets. Not only is life's fortune not to be taken into death, but it can also become the root of misfortune amongst descendants. How lamentable that is! There are others who bustle about, scheming over the smallest chance at profit and going to every extent to accumulate wealth. But when savings are squandered and schemes fall apart, earnings through a life of hard work end up others' to keep. How regrettable that is! Two thousand five hundred years ago, the Buddha already indicated wealth as the sole possession of the five sources — natural disasters, wars, bandits, tyrants, and prodigal offsprings. He thus instructed that donations be made so as to form karmic bonds with each other. A poem describes this perfectly:

> Sow one seed, harvest a hundred;
> Give a dollar, make ten thousand.
> Merits from such good deeds will be
>   locked away in your storehouse,
> Forever to be enjoyed by you and yours.

Despite years of extreme poverty, I have never considered myself to be poor. On the contrary, I see wealth wherever I go: a good word or a good deed, a small convenience or a little friendship ... all are to be treasured. I look upon offerings as auspicious karma, due to come my way in any case but really not warranting any mention. I deeply feel that wealth should resemble water, to be allowed to flow and circulate before it becomes effective. I realize what profound wisdom it is to know how to spend. Most of all, I think it best to expend wealth in ways to let people into the inexhaustible treasure-trove of *prajñā*. This is the only way to the pleasure of wise spending.

And so, I sincerely feel that to possess wealth is auspicious karma, and to spend well, true wisdom.

POVERTY IS
SUCH A CRIME

心甘情願

Upon entering a large, ancient monastery to study, I came to discover people trying to make a statement out of wearing worn-out clothing, or taking to eating rancid rice and leftover vegetables as a form of religious practice. Some even went as far as pretending to be poor and foolish, declaring wealth and fame to be poisonous snakes and fierce beasts and, in doing so, making something lofty out of self-inflicted poverty. One day I heard Venerable Ta Shih, a receptionist serving in the visitor's hall, lament: "Poverty! Poverty! Everyone glorifies poverty. Who will then complete the Pureland's chambers of seven gems, the magnificent world of gold-paved grounds? Poverty is such a crime!"

Poor but Not Self - depreciatory

Those words rang through my ears as if thunder had struck my skull. Back then, catastrophes of war continued without end, and the state of the nation was dire. Not only was social development left neglected and at a standstill, but the monastic economy was also stagnant. Poverty was a national phenomenon.

My master, Venerable Chih K'ai, was at

this time director of Ch'i-hsia Shan Monastery. He never once bemoaned his poverty or complained about his suffering. Quite by contrast, beginning with the opening up of more sources of income and cutting down of expenditures, he set up orchards and vegetable farms, and implemented self-sufficiency through the operation of monastic farming. In addition, he located a charcoal kiln and began a paper mill, and applied manual labor to enhance production. As a result of this self-reliance, Ch'i-hsia Vinaya College and its own Tzung-yang Private Secondary School were later established. Each day we performed our duties arduously, having thin congee, mixed provisions, and bean grounds to satiate our stomachs, and leaving the bean curd and delicacies for devotees and patrons. Upon careful reflection, we had demonstrated through our actions that true poverty is when mental resources are exhausted and degraded! Buddhism must be amply funded to carry out its endeavors and form ties of affinity with all beings. I suddenly realized that poverty *is* the root of crime.

In retrospect, that I was able to see poverty as such a crime had stemmed from childhood experiences. My family, though poor, was one of dignity and integrity. Occasionally, I had to peddle along the street, herd cattle, and pick up garbage to supplement family income. But I felt that being able to help my parents by sharing their anxiety and toil was a matter of honor. I never perceived myself to be inferior because of my poverty.

To please my mother, who had suffered from ill health for a long time, I often told her folk tales. Exploits of the ancients studying assiduously in great adversity as well as maintaining filial loyalty and being chaste left a deep impression on me and became guidelines for my conduct. From my youth, I became cognizant of the fact that poverty and wealth are no more than concepts which depend on each individual's sense of value for their meanings: Poverty in a country, in a society, or among the masses, however, will be the source of endless evil.

Taking the tonsure and entering the monastery at twelve, I discovered a much broader world in Buddhism. As it turned out, the immensity of the universe amounts to more than just heaven and earth, monarchs, relatives, and teachers. The planet that we live on is but a microuniverse within the great chiliocosm of three kinds of thousands of chiliocosms. Other than this life and this world, we have already been transmigrating in the *sahā* world in countless lives within the cycle of existence. Among living beings in the six realms were our fathers, mothers, relatives, and friends in past lives. The zeal shown by all the Buddhas and Bodhisattvas passing through innumerable eons is enough to leave one in awe. I knew not how in many sunsets, the sky completely blanketed with rosy clouds, had I strolled by the river in Chiao Shan, chanting phrases from the sutras to myself: "Mind, the Buddha, all living beings — all nondistinctive in essence." Bit by bit, I realized the truth that "the mind can embrace the unlimited space, and magnanimity can encompass realms as numerous as grains of sand." Within the boundlessness of time and space, I felt myself minute as well as abundant!

Gratefulness is the Greatest Wealth of All

Despite the fact that material life in the monastery was extremely lacking and that the average day was marked by unreasonable commands and ruthless beatings from the elders, it was not for me to complain. On the contrary, I thanked teachers for guiding me into the realm of truth, was grateful for being given a place to live and practice, and appreciated how devotees and supporters from everywhere nurtured my physical body. I was most mindful of the fact that the masses provided us with the necessities of life.

Although the Buddha in the main shrine never said a word to me, and my respected master who gave me tonsure never gave me many words of consolation, I was just as grateful to the Buddha for taking me in with the Dharma and to my master for giving me the life of wisdom. Every morning and night I wondered to myself what accomplishments and what virtues made me worthy of so many blessings. On that, I exerted myself diligently in studies and work. Vowing to offer entire body and mind to the world, I went through religious education with more than my share of the Dharma joy. I felt deeply that we do not need to ask for the material or expect others to bestow tenderness upon us. As long as we know how to be content and grateful and how to make a contribution and bonds of affinity, splendor, honor, and wealth will fill our hearts.

When I left Ta-chüeh Temple, my master's temple on Pai-t'a Shan (White Pagoda Mountain) to take up the post of director at

Hua-ts'ang Temple, I was twenty-two years of age. At the time, the nation was in crisis, the economy was collapsing, and living was incredibly hard. A large sack of cash would exchange for no more than a bottle of oil or a bag of salt. We would always sate ourselves on thick congee three meals daily, only to exhaust all energy in dealing with the conservative senior monks. Although livelihood was extremely meager, we did not despair. We took the rise and fall of Buddhism to be our responsibility. Each and every day was fulfilling. Ideals and ambitions shared in common reflected the inexhaustible resourcefulness of our minds, which inspired us to forget our bodies for the Dharma and sacrifice ourselves for our faith at all costs.

Impermanence Inspires Diligence

When in 1949, barehanded, I came to Taiwan from mainland China, I was as poor as a temple mouse. I had worn the same pair of wooden clogs for two years, and through their soles I could almost see the ground! I wore only a short underrobe which, stitched and patched, was on me for three years. Fellow monastics would rush to hold services and come back with money and gifts. In exhilaration, they would gather around to show off their gains. As for me, to possess even a pen or a piece of paper was incredibly difficult. Some followers sympathized with my poverty, suggesting that I should give up writing articles and submitting manuscripts and go along with the rest of the monastics to engage in services. I was never interested in those. Rather, I always felt a oneness with heaven, earth, and all creatures. As wanting as material wealth might be, the exploit of inner resources was more urgent.

When at daybreak I singlehandedly pulled a wooden cart to the open market to buy vegetables, the twinkling stars and lingering moonlight as well as the roadside foliage and trees were my Dharma companions and spiritual friends. When I sprinkled and swept up dung in the courtyard, in silence I prayed that the masses, too, could sweep away their defilements and mundane filth. When I went outside the monastery to help collect rent, I thanked the mountains, rivers, and earth for letting me gallop and ramble. When I looked after the ill or buried the dead, the message of impermanence made me more aware of what I must do. I must strive unceasingly on the path of Buddhahood. I felt extremely wealthy to find all the phenomena of the universe in the joys of meditation and the Dharma. Through writing, I wanted to share with others the supreme Dharma happiness in my experience.

Although I am very adept at living in accordance with circumstances, I never allow myself to get into a rut or trifle with things in life. When circumstances were ripe, I resolutely left the temple and began struggling in the direction of my aspiration to promote Buddhism. I received disciples, was exposed to great hardships, and spread the Dharma day and night.

In retrospect, only one factor enabled me to create opportunities for Buddhism despite utmost personal poverty: I could not bear to see Buddhism so impoverished! I wanted to elicit a positive change and create a beautiful and prosperous world both for the sake of Buddhism and for all living beings. I wanted all the young people to know that they do not have to accumulate external wealth, but they must excavate the treasure-trove of wisdom within. One can be without wealth and power, but one must strive for the prosperity and strength of the state and society.

Life of Wisdom from
Culture and Education

For years actively speaking on the Dharma and delivering all sentient beings, I have never departed from my obligation to cultural work. With proceeds from my books and the generous sponsorship of followers, I did purchase a fine residence. Writing and reading there became so enjoyable. But to better contribute to the benefit of Buddhism, before long I sold the house and bought the site for Fo Kuang Shan. Despite expending much in the way of financial resources and energy, I enjoyed the fruits of hard work. Despite going deeply into debt, I was always perfectly willing to sacrifice in body and mind for the numerous worlds of the ten directions. And, I never felt poor.

Fo Kuang Shan thirty years ago was an uncultivated mountain area covered by bamboo groves. People criticized me for giving up a good life in the city to go to such a remote and obscure wilderness. But, a feeling of confidence drove me to spread the Dharma and start building schools. After many lean years of blazing trails and clearing paths, struggling against floods, and dealing with uncooperative neighbors, we finally inaugurated Fo Kuang Shan. Nothing on earth is too difficult to accomplish. No amount of paucity need hold one back. Confidence, sincerity, endurance, and perseverance are the most precious forms of wealth; waiting, procrastination, hesitation, and inconsistency are the real roots of poverty. Amitabha Buddha had to uphold the forty-eight vows for numberless eons before the completion of the majestic and splendid Pureland. We must build an abundant and peaceful Pureland among the people. We cannot simply sit and wait for the blessings and revelations of all the Buddhas and Bodhisattvas. We must emulate their compassion and vows of benevolence, and conscientiously work toward creating our own future!

Nothingness Gives Rise to the Wondrous

When I first decided to found the Buddhist college, confidence was the greatest asset. Consequently, I overruled the consensus and got to work. That was how the Buddhist colleges were founded one by one. As more and more Buddhists started coming to the mountain each day, I planned on building shrines to put their minds at ease. Still empty-handed, I told myself that all of society was my wealth. Therefore, relying on the belief of "means coming from all directions will go in all directions," one hall after another were built. Pious men and women making pilgrimages to the Buddhas came in an uninterrupted flow. Not wanting them inconvenienced without food and lodging, I further planned to construct a pilgrimage lodge for them. Yang Tsu-man, who was in charge of finances, repeatedly reported to me that no one was willing to lend us any more funds. But I held fast to my decision, firmly believing that personal credibility and potential support — both financial and spiritual — from followers were wealth in themselves. And now, are we not serving them by adding shrines and branch temples one after another? Poverty is no excuse, for with the Dharma, compassion, wisdom, strength of vows, society, and devotees in mind, nothingness can indeed give rise to the wondrous!

Give to Receive

Often I am asked questions like: "You never went to a teaching school, but how do you engage yourself in education? You never studied architecture, but how do you construct buildings?" True indeed. However, while in the Buddhist college, I began to think how I would teach if I should become involved with education. As I spread the Dharma from mainland China to Taiwan and overseas, I came to appreciate the structure, style, form, and environment of the local architecture. Moreover, I would try to imagine how an engineer should design this or that building or plot a certain land. Thus constantly applying my mind, ideas of what should be done, having already taken form in mind, would come together without effort when circumstances were ripe. If you ask me the key to success, all I can say is that I know how to utilize the bits and pieces of time that I find here and there, and I am mindful of everything going on around me. Resources in the universe are aplenty, providing we have the ingenuity and wisdom to transform them into our wealth. Those who are poor in mind want only to take without making an effort and covet only the ready gains. But the more avaricious they are, the poorer they will become. Has anyone ever seen the greedy and stingy strike wealth? One has to be able to *give* before one can *receive*!

Through the years, I saw a long succession of fellow monastics succumbing to the pressures of hard living. Many lost their direction in fortune and fame. While I mourned their departure I rejoiced for myself. For if in those arduous years I felt sorry for myself, did not work to dig up the treasure-trove within me for motivation, or shortsightedly took to grab at the fortune before my eyes, how would I have been able to uphold the monastic life and my heartfelt aspirations? Having nothing materially is to me a touchstone in life.

Oddly enough, many in our society choose to lean over backwards to eulogize poverty and curse wealth, vying to see who has the least wealth but ending up in a game whereby people turn to chase after fame with a holier-than-thou façade. The fact of the matter is that many earn their wealth which is due them because of their diligence. If society's debasement of wealth were to prevail, it would only hinder social progress.

Untainted Wealth as Sustenance

Notwithstanding the fact that love of money is the root of anxiety and woe, untainted wealth is also the sustenance of studying and practicing Buddhism and the foundation for spreading the Dharma. The Buddha is a proponent of a life of well-being and prosperity. Sure he saw a metaphor in comparing gold to a poisonous snake, but he also advocated earning untainted wealth and possessing an appropriate material life. In *Discourse to Sigāla*, he instructed Sigāla on how to utilize money. In *Amitabha Sutra*, *Medicine Buddha Sutra*, and other classics, he described the Purelands of the Buddhas as being paved with gold and having chambers made of the seven gems. Indeed, Buddhism does not discriminate against any kind of untainted wealth.

Adhering to the Buddha's teachings, I advocate the ideal of "placing wealth among the devotees," and maintain this principle regarding the support from all directions: I do not accept excessive donations from devotees, and I request that followers only donate without any cause for suffering or anguish. Faithful followers of the Dharma must place importance on the needs of their households and careers. I see to it that modern facilities be built so that Buddhist devotees can all practice and progress in a quiet and comfortable environment. On wealth and valuables and the other five desires, neither greed nor refusal is what the Buddha meant by a life of the *middle path*.

I had matured with the growth of Buddhism in Taiwan. Through the years, the deepest unhappiness has been that, like in other communities, wealth in the Buddhist community, far from deficient, suffers much from uneven distribution. Proper utilization of wealth does not lie in how much of it there is, but rather in a proper concept and efficient management. Having wealth but not knowing how to use it is just as poor as poverty. To have wealth is to be fortunate, but to know how to use it is to be wise. The way to revitalize Buddhism lies in its people, wealth, spirituality, and undertakings. "Even an able housewife cannot cook without rice." If there is a deficiency in untainted wealth, it is impossible to accomplish anything. I had personally mapped out guidelines stipulating that a Fo Kuang monastic cannot privately solicit donations, build one's own temples, buy one's own estates, or accumulate one's own wealth. Furthermore, those who manage finances should not possess executive power, and those who have executive power should not manage finances. The senior executives have power, whereas the junior executives take care of finances.

Wealth should be used for the sake of Buddhism and society, not stashed away. People see the resplendent buildings of Fo Kuang Shan go up one after another, but few realize that it is quite common for Fo Kuang Shan not to sustain on overnight provisions and to carry a debt from day to day. But rather than utilizing donations for temples, my greatest joy is in funding for training and education. With more than a thousand monastics spreading Buddhism and lecturing on the Dharma, concentrating on ridding devotees of their misgivings, operating temples, engaging in studies worldwide, becoming well versed in multiple languages, and humanizing, modernizing, and internationalizing Buddhism, devotees of worthy contributions are being repaid with the most invaluable yield! In the same token, monastics publish the Buddhist canon, lexicons, books and periodicals, construct homes for seniors, build kindergartens, provide medical care, and engage in philanthropies too numerous to mention.

Many are not very clear about what is really happening at Fo Kuang Shan. They do not see its contributions to the expansion of the Buddhist faith and the edification of society. They criticize it for being commercialized and moneyed. The fact is not that Fo Kuang Shan has a lot of wealth, but rather that its wealth is all put to good use. Not only is wealth for one year well utilized, but also for the next year and the year after next. As those of us in Fo Kuang Shan live from hand to mouth daily, we take every worthy contribution and expend it only on the Buddhist enterprise of training and education and spreading the Dharma for the benefit of all living beings. We do not pretend to view money as sinful or misplace wealth, and never attempt to stockpile any. Our creed is, on the strength of Buddhism, to build a prosperous and serene Pureland on earth.

Chiliocosms of Prosperity

Someone once said to me: "What a shame you entered the Buddhist order! Or you could have been as wealthy as Wang Yung-ching!" Wang Yung-ching is such an outstanding entrepreneur. How can I compare with him? Monastics such as we are without any real home as soon as we decide to renounce our family abode. As we settle on the Eightfold Noble Path and the six *pāramitās*, we find an abode where there is none; by not living anywhere, we live everywhere. The great chiliocosm of three kinds of thousands of chiliocosms and everything in the universe are in my mind. In this light, with my wealth of the great chiliocosm of three kinds of thousands of chiliocosms, how is Wang Yung-ching able to compare with me? As we monastics, though without any offspring, view everyone with the heart of a parent, all are our children. We may be without any material wealth, but as we utilize the wisdom of *prajñā* and uphold compassion and vows, treasure will be found everywhere. I am deeply grateful to have accumulated such merit and virtue to be allowed into the sangha!

I returned home in 1993 to visit my mother and relatives. President of the Buddhist Association of China, elder Zhao Pu-chu, presented me with a verse. A line ran: "Rich with the great chiliocosm of three kinds of thousands of chiliocosms and honored as the master of all beings." One might say that this encapsulated my self-expectation since becoming a monastic fifty years ago.

THAT BRAVE SIDE OF ME

心甘情願

By nature I would call myself easygoing and modest, and when I was young, this helped gain me the affection of the elders. One day a teacher, Shih, spotted me being picked on by some classmates, and he called out: "Son, you have to rise in the face of challenge! Be brave! For this world belongs to the brave!"

His words became engraved in my mind. In the decades to follow, I had striven in utmost diligence. Looking back now at events of the past, I do feel that I also have a side of me that is brave.

In 1937, with the eruption of the Sino-Japanese war, chaos prevailed throughout China. My home district of Yangchou was no exception: the boom of artillery and fighting in streets and alleys were everywhere, as was the unnerving sight of corpses on pavements. On one occasion I saved a wounded soldier by alerting adults to move him on a broken-down door to the rear. Fleeing danger, I even hid myself among the dead. Barely ten at that time, in the eyes of my family I was seen as possessing smarts and guts far surpassing most. A year later, I, as the third eldest child, accompanied my mother to go in search of my father, who had gone missing on a business trip. In the glow of beacon fires that lit the night, I did not feel the least afraid. Later, upon arriving at Ch'i-hsia Shan, I resolved to become a monastic out of a hasty promise. That was a singular act of courage indeed.

Braving Death for the Buddha's Life of Wisdom

The struggle between the Nationalists and Communists in 1947 was fierce. I was twenty-one and principal of Pai-t'a Primary School. During the day Nationalist troops would storm the school in search of the Communists; at night Communist guerrillas would stage surprise counterattacks on the Nationalists. Most every day was a repeat of the last, as we commoners, squeezed perilously in the vise of the two opposing forces, eked out a daily existence. But it never frightened me much.

In those days Buddhism was so infested with multiple problems of its own that even its very continuation was at stake, not to mention its function in aiding the needy and delivering the suffering. In view of this, a class of young monastics and I got together in Ihsing to found the Buddhist *Nu-t'ao* (Raging Billows) magazine, traveled to Hsüchou to produce *Hsia-kuang* (Crimson Glow) bimonthly, and proceeded to Sungchiang to put up posters, distribute leaflets, and lecture at street corners — all in the cause of a new and revolutionary Buddhism that had taken strides out of the mountain monasteries and into society. Undaunted by the potent resistance of conservative elements, we rode on the zeal to revive Buddhism: the greater the frustration, the stronger our courage.

Arriving in 1948 at Hua-ts'ang Temple in Nanjing, the abbot, Venerable Yin Yün, was gracious enough to turn the entire temple over to us for supervision. But it was not long before we recognized how the temple was mired in problems. Wasting no time, we applied ourselves to extensive changes, implementing new regulations to govern life in the order and revamping the institution of Buddhist rituals. We had not, however, anticipated that friction with the senior monastics would intensify from day to day, or that our progressive thinking would come to offend not only warlords and politicians, but also land-owners and community leaders. Subsequently, the reactionary monks and bureaucrats banded together against us. Venerable Chu Yün once took a ferocious beating, and Venerables Sung Fêng and Sung Ch'üan almost perished in the hands of street mobs. As for myself, who held the position of director, the possibility of being killed was literally around every corner. But I was not in the least scared. I felt instead a powerful sense of mission and the urge to give all for the sake of my faith. Constant thoughts of historical role models abound: T'an Szŭ-t'ung, one of six famed martyrs at the end of the Ch'ing dynasty, and revolutionaries Ch'iu Chin and Lin Chüeh-min, who had sacrificed their own lives as well as the happiness of their families for the salvation of the masses. Being a monastic, if I balked at sacrificing myself for Buddhism and universally benefiting all sentient beings, how could I possibly succeed?

In 1949, China was in ruins. I made a pact with Venerable Chih Yung: for Buddhism's sake, one of us had to stay to continue sowing its seeds and furthering the Buddha's life of wisdom. It was decided that he would stay behind and I would go to Taiwan. Having lived all my life deep in interior China, I knew precious little about the rest of the world. Even the impression I had of Taiwan, based on long outdated source texts, was one of a place that was savage, uncultivated, and disease-ridden. I thought to myself: did not Great Master Hsüan Tsang also face the perils of flowing deserts and fierce beasts all on his own when traveling west to fetch the sutras? Ancient sages also said, "For the sake of a great undertaking, how can one fret over putting one's life at risk!" So, without the slightest hesitation, I headed on my own for Taiwan, where the people and customs were to me totally alien. After a roundabout route to Ilan, I began propagating the Dharma. Later on, without knowing much about Taiwan at all, I proceeded to tour the island alone. Some years later, without any knowledge of the English language, I even ventured overseas a few times on my own. In retrospect, it was on the strength of resolve and courage that, as a naive and inexperienced youth, I was able to face a strange environment and an uncertain future barehanded.

Initially without any relatives in Taiwan, I looked in all directions for a place to stay. I repeatedly encountered rejection and was mocked on numerous occasions. With the discontinuation of regular meals, hunger and cold were my unrelenting companions. However, not once was I discouraged. A lady, Sun-Chang Ching-yang, treated me with great respect and offered to send me abroad to study. Penniless as I was, I had never thought of accepting, let alone felt the need to ever complain to her of my poverty or beg her for patronage. With no funds, contacts, or furniture in my shabby little cubicle, I was eventually able to take it upon myself to launch a college for eager young intellectuals. Some of those outstanding youths who came around at the time included Wu I, Chang Shang-te, and Wang Shang-i, all participants of the first Buddhist youth seminar that I held.

In 1967, after going in all directions to raise funds for the property purchase for Fo Kuang Shan, I was left with a paltry sum for clearing and construction projects. For many, that was an outright fantasy. However, the splendid structures crowning Fo Kuang Shan today are proofs of how courage is able to overpower wealth.

Fearless of Evils in Spreading the Right Belief

Taiwan thirty to forty years ago was bound by traditions. In an effort to promote Buddhist propriety and to do away with the practice of worshiping with live animals common among the populace, I took to innovations such as Buddhist choirs, slide presentations, children's sunday schools, student bodies, and traveling groups. These new approaches, however, brought endless objections and criticisms, to the point of vicious name-calling and death threats. Rather than taken aback, I continued to act as a vanguard of innovative preaching by recording, broadcasting, and incorporating variety programs into Buddhist festivities. As voices of opposition surged forth like tidal waves, I clung to my aspirations and had not for once wavered.

Buddhist temples today continue to practice the same models in promoting the Dharma, indicating how imperative that initial courage is in an innovative commitment. Later on, the Buddha's birthday float parade, the islandwide Buddhist canon propagation group, and other modern evangelist activities instigated waves of fervent interest in Buddhism. Upon recollection, caught back then in the circumstances of our own inexperience and the animosity from both within and without our religious circle, we triumphed in that we had only our own confidence and courage to fall back on.

Spreading the Dharma is certainly not without its many trials and tribulations, just as building monasteries and founding schools are not without their manifold obstacles. Once in 1965, I was at Shou-shan Temple eagerly announcing plans to found a Buddhist college, when an influential devotee tried to dampen my spirits, saying: "Master! If you insist on a

Buddhist college which we cannot hope to
fund for the long term, soon you will have to
go without food!" In all honesty, we were
extremely short on resources, but then in
training the sangha, I was just as convinced in
that we could not afford to stand idle for a
moment longer. Not flinching in the least at
any of the threats and warnings, I resolutely
went ahead with my goals. As a result,
graduates from the Buddhist college have
numbered in the thousands in the last thirty
years. Those who enrolled early at the
beginning, such as Tzu Chia, Tzu Yi, Yi Yen,
Hsin Ting, Yi Heng, and Hsin Ju, have all
distinguished themselves in their services at
Fo Kuang Shan. If at any point I had been the
slightest hesitant, many Buddhist leaders and
fine talents would have been lost for no good
reason at all.

Fundraising for Fo Kuang Shan was also
met with plenteous oppositions. Many felt that
Lei-yin Temple in Ilan and Shou-shan Temple
in Kaohsiung would suffice for worship. Why
bother with yet another temple? Subsequently,
I rented a large bus with the express purpose
of taking everybody to the site, hoping to
explain my ideals there and then. Little would
I have expected that upon setting their eyes
on the thorny bushes, bamboo-covered

mountain, and inaccessible grassy areas, people would become even more apprehensive. Some even refused to get off the bus, saying: "Who would come to a spooky place like this? If you want, Venerable, go by yourself!" I disembarked by myself and strolled around the foot of the mountain. After giving it all careful consideration, in profound decisiveness I told myself: "As for me, there's no way I am not coming to this mountain!"

During the time that was spent clearing the mountain, the endless toiling away, wave upon wave of physical strain, the planning that carried on into all hours of the day, the barrage of floods and other natural disasters, and the belligerent mobs that surrounded the mountain were all quite beyond description. However, in the momentum of an incomparable courage and by the blood and sweat of the laborers, the vast wilderness was transformed into the scenic Fo Kuang Shan today. And, those who would not budge in the bus that day became regular pilgrims of the mountain. The construction of Hsi Lai Temple later in Los Angeles also encountered opposition from the neighborhood. More than a hundred public hearings and meetings and ten years of arduous labor later, it stands as the largest Buddhist temple in the western hemisphere, much to the growing respect of the American people. As the other branch temples around the world were founded amidst economic pressures and shortages of manpower, it would be impossible to recount the hardship in the coming about of these temples. If not for this fierce self-confidence and willpower of ours, there is no way that our aspiration of "the Buddha's light shining across the great chiliocosm of three kinds of thousands of chiliocosms, and the water of the Dharma flowing across the five continents" could have been realized. As for me, retirement from Fo Kuang Shan would only mean devotion to Buddha's Light International Association.

All my life I have been easygoing and lived in accordance with the circumstances, but in matters of the principle, I would absolutely never compromise! When I took over the management of Lei-yin Temple, I had asked — with many glaring eyes cast upon me — that some inappropriate icons be removed. To add fuel to the fire, I personally chopped up the two "Make Way" signs that were used in parades. I did so for the sanctity and dignity of the temple. Another time, as a member of the Maitreya scholarship evaluation committee, I protested to Venerable Nan Ting, the director, about the inappropriateness in distribution by pounding on the table. During construction of Kaohsiung Buddhist Temple, I was aware of a *sauvastika* on a wall, which is incongruous with orthodox Buddhism. Much against the consensus, I had the structure torn down and then rebuilt! Later it would be proven such a decision was correct. Furthermore, I insisted that the two enormous stone lions in front of the shrine of the Buddha be smashed. This time, those devotees who had been critical of me vowed to protect the lions. But when they saw me sitting upright, eyes closed, and unruffled, they yielded and dispersed in silence. The temple completed, I voluntarily stepped down as director and cordially invited the senior monk, Venerable Yüeh Chi, to be abbot. For quite some time, proceedings at the temple in Kaohsiung were met with a lot of obstructions. Disturbances from other religions were not infrequent. But I let them be and, after a while, they left us alone.

As a young monastic in training at a large temple, I would read with hearty admiration about the sages of antiquity and their selflessness toward Buddhism. The courageous exploits of Venerable Chih Shih of the T'ang dynasty, who, over the issue of seating precedence involving a Buddhist monastic and a Taoist, was willing to be caned in defiance of the emperor, earned my respect most. I vowed to emulate his intrepidity. I remember well an experience we had during Taiwan's martial law period. I was hauled into the police station for violating the ban in Hualian. Once there, however, I protested vehemently, saying to the officers: "We have virtually been everywhere propagating religion. Not once were we prohibited to do so by anybody. Is Hualian somewhere on the fringe of civilization?" They were flabbergasted by my stentorian sternness. On another occasion, I was in Lungtan speaking on the Dharma when I spotted the police making arrests offstage. Without the slightest misgivings, I remained on stage and carried on with my lecture. To my disbelief, the police and myself, without becoming involved with each other's affairs, remained at peace to the end. In Ilan, the police repeatedly received anonymous letters claiming that I received radio broadcasts from China in the day and changed attire to go putting up Communist slogans or passing out leaflets at night. Things got to such absurdity that the police was informed of Fo Kuang Shan stashing away ammunition. These false accusations could

have given me enough reasons to fear for my
life at all times, but I have never shied away
from traveling in all directions to spread the
Dharma — just as before.

Intrepidly Defending Faith, History is My Model

Thirty years ago, when Shou-shan Temple had
just been built, the authorities attempted to
order its demolition on the height of its
building. As I saw it, circumstances already
made it difficult enough for the devotees in
Kaohsiung to find a spiritual sanctuary, so how
could I just sit by and let this temple be leveled
to the ground? I spoke so sternly and forcefully
in the cause of justice that the official in charge
took to a long string of apologies and revoked
the order.

I spoke often in the name of justice about
unfair government measures against
Buddhism. In their place, I would offer many
constructive opinions. I recommended the
replacement of regulated supervision of
monasteries with a law for religious equality.
In 1963, persecution against Buddhism in
Vietnam caused an international uproar.
Despite Taiwan's ban of public discussion of
the religious circumstances in Vietnam, I took

it upon myself to write in denunciation of the atrocity. Involvement in heated verbal exchanges is what I am always loath to do, which can bring about such obstacles. However, that the teachings of Buddhism can be passed forever on through time is indebted to practitioners' efforts in issues of right and wrong, not of gains and losses. How can I alone face history in shame?

Not only have I dedicated my endeavors to religious justice, but I have also undertaken to safeguard social justice. Many a time I would offer refuge to persons believed to be publicly wronged or falsely implicated. In so doing, I would be putting my own life on the line. Many a righteous and outspoken scholar would be invited to lecture at Fo Kuang Shan, which was once called an enemy base of some sort. All I know is that I am upholding human rights, trying to mend political squabbles, and treating scholars with due respect. In the name of justice, I am merely doing what must be done.

When the former president Chiang Kai-shek passed away, I presented a speech criticizing the religious bias in his will. I once proposed to the former president Chiang Ching-kuo the opening up of channels of communication with government. When president Lee Teng-hui first took office, I expressed disapproval over his making a public testimonial of his Christian faith. For the betterment of Taiwan, I am willing to admonish the authorities without reserve. And, I would like to think it all to have stemmed from an abundance of courage.

In the last few years I have taken the lead in returning to mainland China to spread the Dharma and to visit relatives. Prominent figures such as Xu Jia-tun and Qian Jia-ju and those individuals active in the democracy movement I have received as honored guests. This high profile of mine has won me as much accolade as criticism. The "political monk" have I been labeled these days, but I would have no cause for complaints or regrets. As I see it, benevolence and tolerance are the most effective keys to peace among humankind. As such, I promise to work untiringly toward bringing both sides of the Strait of Taiwan in respect, peace, and solidarity.

In *Fo i-chiao ching* (Sutra of the Buddha's Last Instruction), it is stated:

> Those able to practice forbearance are deemed individuals of tremendous power. If, on the other hand, one is unable to joyfully endure the evil, venomous cursing of others as the drinking of sweet

dew, then one cannot be called a person
of penetrating wisdom.

Forty years ago, in writing *Shih-chia-mou-ni Fo ch'uan* (Biography of Sakyamuni Buddha), I already got a taste of what the Buddha meant by these words. It so happened that during a board meeting at the Tzu-ai Kindergarten, a devotee suddenly suggested that somebody who had nothing to do with the proceedings should preside. I was about to walk offstage when a teacher exploded in rage, pounding on the table and cursing: "What a bunch of hellish seeds! It was the master who founded the Buddhist kindergarten, and now you have the unbelievable gall to replace him with somebody else!" The devotee who had made the first move caved in completely while I was asked to resume the role of chairperson. I did not really relish the idea of going back on stage, but thought to myself there and then: "If not me, then who else? When in the right, never yield." Putting aside the humiliation of having been driven offstage, I walked back on to continue to preside over the meeting. Who would have known how much courage was needed to do this! My profound realization was that tolerance is the greatest force on earth.

Approaching the age of seventy, I turn my head to look back on the dust that I have stirred on the road behind me: decade upon decade of worrying both for my country and my faith and of spreading the Dharma for the benefit of all sentients. I have had my share of ridicule, but have remained resolute in my forbearance. Despite obstacles and hardships, I have managed to press on with courage. I am only ashamed that my efforts still fall short by a considerable margin when compared to how Kou-chien of the Yüeh kingdom goaded himself ahead by self-deprivation. When placed alongside all the Buddhas and Bodhisattvas, who eradicate suffering, bring about joy, and work in diligence for hundreds of eons, all I can do is watch in astonishment, my own achievements paling in comparison. I only hope that in the days to come, there will be more and greater hardships, so that I may harden in mind and body, and accept more suffering on behalf of the masses. Only then will my vows be truly fulfilled!